WOMEN'S STUDIES

A Guide To Reference Sources

Kathleen Burke McKee

With a supplement on feminist serials in The University of Connecticut Library's Alternative Press Collection, by Joanne V. Akeroyd

With the assistance of B. McIlvaine, Government Publications Department

The University of Connecticut Library, Storrs
Bibliography Series, Number 6

Copyright 1977 by The University of Connecticut.

Library of Congress Cataloging in Publication Data
McKee, Kathleen Burke.
Women's studies.

(Bibliography series; no 6)
Includes indexes.
1. Women's studies—bibliography—catalogs.
2. Connecticut. University. Library. I. McIlvaine, B., joint author. II. Akeroyd,
Joanne V. III. Title. IV. Series: Bibliography series (Storrs, Conn.); no. 6
Z7965.M33 [HQ1181.U5] 016.30141'2 77-1747
ISBN 0-917590-01-5

FORWARD

Women's studies is an academic program devoted to the pursuit of knowledge about women. The curriculum draws on the scholarship that has developed in the context of feminist ideology. Focus in the discipline is on an examination of myths, images, and assumptions about women, a search for new knowledge, and the development of new theories and methods of analysis.

Women's studies also provides students with an academic experience which is related to their personal lives and an opportunity to learn of the possibilities open to them in a society not limited by stereotyped views of the role of the sexes. Thus women's studies contributes to the full utilization of human potential in personal, community, and occupational roles.

Women's studies courses focus on: an examination of myths and literature for the biases, subtle and blatant, that have affected academic disciplines in the study of women; the teaching about and encouragement of new research on women and their contributions to our cultural heritage; application of the results of feminist social analysis to teaching and to efforts to change the role and status of women in society; the merits of an interdisciplinary approach to the study of women; and participation in the evolution of a new knowledge base and a revision of the value of the feminine mode in intellectual and interpersonal life.

It is clear that students, teachers, and scholars in women's studies and others interested in the new scholarship on women will find this guide to reference sources of great value in their work.

Martha Mednick, Director
Women's Studies Program
The University of Connecticut
February, 1977

3

INTRODUCTION

The seventies have brought an information explosion in the field of women's studies, and with this explosion, a need to control and access the literature of a new discipline. This bibliography is intended to be a guide to the new reference sources which deal with women's studies and also to reference sources from more traditional disciplines which are useful in women's studies research. The bibliography is based on the collection of the University of Connecticut Library, Storrs, although many of the items listed may be found in other large research libraries as well. It is hoped that the bibliography will prove a helpful introduction for the women's studies researcher.

Items included are arranged by type of publication, and are indexed by author, title, and subject. Annotations give purpose, arrangement, and use of the sources in women's studies research. Subject indexing terms are listed, as these vary widely from source to source; they also further illustrate the use of a particular item in women's studies.

A selected number of government publications have been included in the bibliography. Additional documents may be located by using the indexes to government publications listed in this bibliography and by consulting librarians in the Government Publications Department.

The Alternative Press Collection's feminist reference books are included in the main section of the bibliography. A special supplement listing feminist serials appears at the end. Many of these were included in *Alternatives; a guide to the newspapers, magazines, and newsletters in the Alternative Press Collection in the Special Collections Department of the University of Connecticut Library*, by Joanne V. Akeroyd. 2d ed. Storrs, Ct.: The University of Connecticut Library, April, 1976. (Bibliography Series, no. 5), but were not annotated. In addition to these reference books and periodicals, the collection contains a growing number of books and pamphlets from movement publishers on third world women, socialist feminism, lesbianism, health collectives, and other feminist issues. Many of these books and pamphlets are listed in the card catalog, but some are not yet cataloged, or are listed only in the Special Collections Department's Alternative Press Collection catalog. The reader is encouraged to ask for assistance in the department.

Call numbers and locational symbols have been added to the listings to aid in locating the items in the University of Connecticut Library. These are:

Ref.	Reference Department
GPD	Government Publications Department

GPD RR   Government Publications Department,
Reading Room
Spec.   Special Collections Department

I would like to thank the members of the Reference, Government Publications, and Special Collections Departments for their support and encouragement, the Women's Studies Program for continued interest in the project, and Sandra Beaupre, Frances Horila, and Elizabeth Nyberg for their kind assistance in typing the manuscript. Special thanks must go to Valerie Ralston, whose editorial assistance was invaluable in completing the bibliography, and to my husband Richard, for his patience.

Kathleen Burke McKee
January, 1977

Table of Contents

GUIDES

1 Krichmar, Albert.
  Women's Studies. Santa Barbara, Calif.: University Library,
  University of California at Santa Barbara, 1975.
  <u>Ref. Z7961.K75 1975b</u>
  Partially annotated guide to the women's studies collection at
  the University of California at Santa Barbara Library. Includes
  bibliographies dealing with women, selected periodical and
  newspaper indexes, biographical sources, library catalogs, and
  directories. Also included are bibliographies of books on
  women in various subject fields, and books on foreign and
  minority women. Brief lists of women's periodicals and
  government documents are included.

2 Lynn, Naomi, Ann B. Matasar and Marie Barovic Rosenberg.
  Research Guide in Women's Studies. Morristown, N.J.:
  General Learning Press, 1974.
  <u>Ref. HQ1206.L96</u>

  Guide which gives much general information on how to write
  a research paper, gather statistics, conduct interviews, etc.
  Some information is given on reference sources, but few are
  related specifically to women's research. Indexed by subject.

3 Pathfinders.
  Reading, Mass.: Addison-Wesley Publishing Co., 1972-   .
  <u>Ref. Desk</u>

  Single page, basic guides to appropriate sources for a student
  beginning library research in an unfamiliar area. Pertinent
  women's areas covered thus far include:
  Anthropology   — Nuclear family
                    — Rites of passage
  Education   — Sex education

Political Science	— Woman suffrage
Literature	— Emily Dickinson
	— Sylvia Plath
	— Virginia Woolf
Sociology	— Abortion—Social and legal aspects
	— Prostitution—U.S.—20th century
	— Rape
	— Witchcraft
	— Women's liberation—U.S.

4   Schlachter, Gail and Donna Belli.

The Changing Role of Women in America: a selected annotated bibliography of references sources. Monticello, Ill., 1975. (Council of Planning Librarians Exchange Bibliography, no. 931)   Ref. Z5942.C68 no. 931

Lists sources focusing on women in America. Author and title indexes.

5   Wheeler, Helen Rippier.

Womanhood Media. Metuchen, N.J.: Scarecrow Press, 1972.
_____ Supplement, 1975.   Ref. Z7961.W48

Compendium of resources on women. Part I is a women's liberation awareness test. Part II describes standard reference sources useful in researching women's topics. Part III is a basic book collection on women which can be used as a guide to reading on women's issues. Part IV lists non-book resources, including audio-visual resources, pamphlets, movement periodicals, and special issues of periodicals devoted to women. Part V is a directory of sources listing organizations, publishers, information centers, speakers, and women's groups. The supplement updates parts III, IV, and V.

LIBRARY CATALOGS AND COLLECTIONS

6 Arthur and Elizabeth Schlesinger Library on the History of Women in America.

> The Manuscript Inventories and Catalogues of Manuscripts, Books, and Pictures, Radcliffe College, Cambridge, Mass. Boston: G. K. Hall, 1973. 3v. Ref. Z881.C33

> Catalog of one of the largest collections of source material on the history of American women from 1800 to the present. The collection includes papers of suffrage leaders, family archives, books, periodicals, newsletters, journals, newspapers, task force reports, microfilms, tapes, TV scripts, and other research data collected by the library at Radcliffe College. The first two volumes are a book catalog arranged by author, title, and subject, with a special section on the etiquette collection and a listing of periodicals. The third volume is a manuscript inventory and catalog of the picture collection.

7 Harvard University. Peabody Museum of Archaeology and Ethnology. Library.

> Catalogue: Authors. Boston: G. K. Hall, 1963. 26v.
> ———. Supplement. 1st, 1970; 2nd, 1971; 3rd, 1975.
>   Ref. Z5119.H35

> Catalogue: Subjects. Boston: G. K. Hall, 1963. 27v.
> ———. Index to Subject Headings, 1963. rev. ed., 1971.
> ———. Supplement. 1st, 1970; 2nd, 1971; 3rd, 1975.
>   Ref. Z5119.H36

> Catalog of an outstanding collection in the field. Important feature is the inclusion of selected journal articles as well as books and other types of publications. The subject catalog is arranged geographically with topical subdivisions. Headings used include: linguistics—woman's language; sociology—woman; somatology—woman; women.

8 Smith College. Library.
Catalogs of the Sophia Smith Collection: Women's History
Archive, Smith College. Boston: G. K. Hall, 1975.
Ref. Z7965.S542

Catalog of the nation's oldest archive of women's history.
Manuscript, printed and iconographic sources document the
history of women from 1795. Emphasis is on U.S. women.
Author, subject, and manuscript sections.

9 Women's History Research Center, Inc.
Herstory. Berkeley, California, 1971.
Micro/Media Dept.
Reel Guide—Ref. Dept.

The microfilmed periodical collection of the Women's History
Research Center through September, 1971. Over three hundred
titles are represented, including women's liberation
newspapers and newsletters and some women's civic,
religious, professional, and peace journals. Unfortunately,
there is no index, only a reel guide, and for many titles only a
few issues have been filmed. The Women's History Research
Center itself has been disbanded due to lack of funds and
materials sent to various libraries. The subject files and
organizational archives are at the University of Wyoming, the
serials at Northwestern University, pamphlets at Princeton,
films at the University of California at Berkeley Art Museum,
and other archives at Radcliffe College. The Center's
collections on *Women and Health/Mental Health* and
Women and Law and an update of *Herstory* to 1974 have been
microfilmed and are available for purchase from Northeast
Micrographics, Branford, Ct.

In order to locate other library collections dealing with women,
consult the following sources:

10 Ash, Lee.
Subject Collections. 4th ed. N.Y.: Bowker, 1974.
Ref. Z731.A78 1974

Guide to special collections and subject emphases of academic,
public, and special libraries in the U.S. and Canada. Notes are
given on special features of collections, size, and availability
for loan and photocopy. Listings are arranged under subject
headings, by state, city, and library. Relevant headings
include: education of women; woman; woman-rights of

women; woman-social and moral questions; woman-suffrage; women; women, American; women as authors; women as laborers; women as physicians; women in business; women in management; women in medicine; women in professions; Women's Army Corps (WACS); Women's International League for Peace and Freedom; women's liberation movement.

11 Young, Margaret Labash, Harold Chester Young and Anthony T. Kruzas, eds.

Directory of Special Libraries and Information Centers. 3rd. ed. Detroit: Gale Research Co., 1974. 3v.

Ref. Z731.Y68 1974

Volume one is the directory proper with a subject index at the end. Volume two is a geographic and personnel index. Volume three is a periodical supplement, *New Special Libraries*, which will appear four times until the next cumulation. Listings in the directory are arranged alphabetically by name of library. Information given includes address, founding date, staff, subjects covered, publications, and number of holdings. There are separate sections for libraries in the U.S. and in Canada. Women and suffrage are used as terms in the subject index.

Subject Directory of Special Libraries and Information Centers. 3rd. ed. Detroit: Gale Research Co., 1975.

Ref. Z675.A2 Y68

A compilation of the above directory by broad subject fields.

HANDBOOKS

GENERAL

12 Boston Women's Collective, Inc.
    Women's Yellow Pages; the original source book for women.
    2nd. ed. Boston, Mass.: The Collective, 1973.

    <u>Spec. XA I.6 no. 60</u>

    A combination of resource directories, factual essays, and
    peptalks for women in the Boston area who need advice or
    assistance with children, education, employment, food and
    nutrition, health, aging, legal matters, media, money,
    self-defense, and welfare. Directory of women's groups in
    Massachusetts and index included.

13 Grimstad, Kirsten, and Susan Rennie, eds.
    The New Woman's Survival Sourcebook. New York, N.Y.:
    Knopf, 1975.   <u>Spec. C2880</u>

    First published in 1973, this thoroughly updated edition
    covers work, money, health, lifestyles, children and youth,
    sports, education, literature, communications, the arts,
    religion and spirituality, law and politics, violence against
    women, men, movement history, and trends. Lists, complete at
    the time of publication, of presses, periodicals, bookstores,
    health clinics, rape crisis centers, and hotlines. Includes
    illustrations, bibliographies, essays, and index.

14 U.S. Women's Bureau.
    International Documents on the Status of Women.
    Washington, D.C.: U.S.G.P.O., 1947. (Women's Bureau
    Bulletin, no. 217)   <u>GPD L13.3:217</u>

    Chronology and collection of excerpts on the status of women
    in documents of the League of Nations and the United

Nations. Although there is no bibliography or index, this would be a good starting point for research.

15 Women's Rights Almanac.
    N.Y.: Harper and Row, 1974-   . Ref. HQ1426.W665 1974

    Compilation of statistics, organizations, and facts concerning women in areas such as politics, legal rights, employment, family, health, and many more. A state-by-state breakdown, a section on national resources and information, brief analytical essays on major issues in the movement, and a chronology of the movement are given. Indexed.

HEALTH

16 Boston Women's Health Book Collective.
    Our Bodies, Ourselves: a Book by and for Women. 2nd. ed.
    New York: Simon and Schuster, 1976.
                                    Spec. C3010

    Topics include self-awareness, sexuality, lesbianism, health and nutrition, rape, self-defense, abortion, childbearing and parenthood, menopause, health care. Contains quotes of personal experiences, summaries of important studies, accepted and alternative practices or methods of treatment, suggestions for action, and often extensive bibliographies. Includes index. See also first edition (Spec. C2215).

LABOR

17 Organize! A Working Women's Handbook.
    Berkeley, Calif.: UNION W.A.G.E. Educational Committee,
    1975.   Spec. XA I.6 no. 61

    Written chiefly for women clericals. Sections include: How to Organize a Union; Writing and Negotiating Your Union Contract; Learning the Rules and Building a Caucus; Bibliography.

18 U.S. Women's Bureau.
    Handbook on Women Workers, 1975. Washington, D.C.:
    U.S.G.P.O., 1976. (Women's Bureau Bulletin, no. 297)
                                    GPD L36.103:297

    Major reference source of textual matter and statistics. Divided into three parts: women in the labor force; laws governing women's employment and status; and institutions and mechanisms to advance the status of women. The latter part describes accomplishments of each program or agency. There is a detailed table of contents and a subject index. Earlier editions of the handbook are also available as Women's Bureau Bulletins: first edition, 1948 (no. 225), 1950 (no. 237), 1952 (no. 242), 1954 (no. 255), 1956 (no. 261), 1958 (no. 266), 1960 (no. 275), 1962 (no. 285), 1965 (no. 290), 1969 (no. 294). The first three issues were titled *Handbook of Facts on Women Workers*.

LAW

19   California. Commission on the Status of Women.
A Commentary on the Effect of the Equal Rights Amendment on State Laws and Institutions, prepared by Anne K. Bingaman. Sacramento: Commission on the Status of Women, 1975. GPD 5-St3.2:Eq2/1

Although written in California, commentary is not limited to that state's laws. Effect of the ERA is expressed in terms general enough to apply in all states. Individual chapters deal with: the ERA and the Constitution, criminal laws and penal institutions, education, family laws, labor laws, and marital property laws. There are short bibliographies scattered throughout. Also contains a table of cases, and subject index.

20   Hanna, John Paul.
The Complete Layman's Guide to the Law. Englewood Cliffs, N.J.: Prentice Hall, 1974. Ref. KF387.H28

This compilation of legal definitions can be of use to the layperson in gaining an understanding of the basic legal structure. It does not, however, give references to the law it is citing. Also, it is difficult for any legal book to be current and "complete," as the law changes rapidly. Nonetheless, this book does have information on a variety of legal matters of interest in women's studies. These include: abortion; equal employment; family law (marriage, divorce, child custody, etc.); prostitution; rape, etc.

21   Women Behind Bars; an organizing tool.
Washington, D.C.: Resources for Community Change, 1975.
Spec. XA I.6 no. 57

Begins with the premises that the prison system is a failure and that women prisoners have the added crippling burden of sexism, and provides information and organizing material not previously available for women prisoners. Sections include articles (analyses, strategies, overview); groups (support and service groups, special programs, prisoners' unions, legal aid and bail information, re-entry and halfway houses, prostitution); resources (books, articles, films, tapes, etc. on organizing, legal and drug resources, personal accounts, general prison resources, bibliographies). Indexes by subject, group, resources, and state.

DIRECTORIES

BIOGRAPHICAL DIRECTORIES AND INDEXES

22   American Men and Women of Science.
  13th ed. N.Y.: Bowker, 1976. 7v. Ref. Biog. Q141.A47

  Covers prominent American scientists. Divided into two sections, one for the physical and biological sciences, and one for the social and behavioral sciences. Alphabetically arranged including personal data, education, positions held, memberships, field of research interest, and address.

23   American Physical Society. Committee on Women in Physics.
  Women in Physics; a roster. N.Y.: Published for the American Physical Society by the American Institute of Physics, 1972.
    Ref. Biog. QC16.2.A44

  Lists women physicists, including field of research interest, degrees, and employer.

24   American Women; the official who's who among the women of the nation.
  Los Angeles: Richard Blank Publishing Co. v.2, 1937/38; v.3, 1939/40.   Ref. Biog. E747.A69

  Leaders in many fields living during the period of publication are listed. Data includes personal biographical information and achievements. Geographical and occupational indexes are included as well as a statistitcal summary of facts concerning the group of women listed. Statistics cover age, education, politics, marital status, hobbies, and leisure activities. Volume three updates the information on the women listed in volume two and includes additional women.

25   Biography Index.
  N.Y.: H. W. Wilson, 1946-   . v.1-   . Quarterly.
    Ref. Biog. Z5301.B5

Covers biographical material appearing in books, periodicals, *New York Times* obituaries, individual and collective biographies, and incidental biographical material in otherwise nonbiographical books. References are arranged alphabetically by name of person with an index by profession and occupation. "Wives of prominent men" is a category here, although there is no corresponding section for husbands of prominent women.

26   Contemporary Authors.
       Detroit: Gale Research, 1962- . v.1- .
                           Ref. Biog. Z1224.C6

       _____. 1st. rev. Detroit: Gale Research, 1967- . v.1- .
                           Ref. Biog. Z1224.C59

Bio-bibliographical guide to living authors, mostly writing in English. Each listing gives personal data, career, works in progress, criticism, and a bibliography of works. Cumulative index available to volumes 1-56, which also indexes the companion series, *Contemporary Literary Criticism.*

27   Current Biography.
       N.Y.: H. W. Wilson, 1940- . v.1- . Monthly.
                           Ref. Biog. CT100.C8

Biographical articles on people prominent in the news. Information includes personal data, occupation, reason for newsworthiness, biographical sketch with portrait, and references to additional biographical material on the person. Includes classified occupation list and necrology section listing obituaries of people previously covered who have died. Approximately 300-350 individuals are covered each year. Cumulates yearly into the *Current Biography Yearbook*, and there is a cumulative index to persons covered 1940-1970.

28   Engelbarts, Rudolf.
       Women in the United States Congress, 1917-1972. Littleton, Colorado: Libraries Unlimited, 1974.
                           Ref. Biog. JK1030.A2 E5

An attempt to summarize the congressional careers of women who have served in the House and Senate. Useful information on legislation sponsored, committee positions held, and voting scores is provided. Arrangement is chronological by year of arrival in Congress. Bibliographies on each individual refer the reader to further sources of information. There are also bibliographies on women in politics and related topics. Indexed by name and subject.

29 Foremost Women in Communications.
N.Y.: Foremost Americans Publishing Corp., 1970.
Ref. Biog. P92.5.A1 F6

Covers accomplished women in broadcasting, advertising, public relations, library science, journalism, publishing, and marketing. Information on education, career, and achievements is submitted by the women themselves. Arrangement is alphabetical, with geographical and subject indexes.

30 Ireland, Norma Olin.
Index to Women of the World from Ancient to Modern Times; biographies and portraits. Westwood, Mass.: F. W. Faxon Co., 1970.   Ref. Biog. Z7963.B6 I73

This index to 945 collective biographies provides excellent access to material on little known women in history. Alphabetic in arrangement, with birth and death date, nationality, occupation, and references to biographical sketches and portraits which appear in the collections analyzed for each of the women listed. List of collections analyzed with complete bibliographical information is given at the beginning of the volume. The introduction gives an overview of women's contributions in history, with special emphasis on women as pioneers, women as patriots and military leaders, women in fine arts and literature, and women in science.

31 Jourcin, Albert and Ph. Van Tieghem.
Dictionnaire des Femmes Célèbres. Paris: Larousse, 1969.
Ref. Biog. CT3203.J68

Brief biographies, in French, of celebrated women from many nations. The time period covered ranges from ancient to modern, but mythological figures and those whose historical existence is uncertain have been eliminated. Many of the entries are illustrated with photographs, portraits, or sculptures of the women.

32 Kulkin, Mary-Ellen.
Her Way; biographies of women for young people. Chicago:

American Library Association, 1976.

Ref. Biog. HQ1123.K75

Bio-bibliography; includes annotated lists of recommended, non-sexist children's biographies. Individual, geographical, and occupational indexes.

33 Notable American Women, 1607-1950; A biographical dictionary. Ed. by Edward T. James. Cambridge, Mass.: Belknap Press of Harvard University Press, 1971. 3v.

Ref. Biog. CT3260.N57

An excellent collection of biographical sketches of approximately thirteen hundred distinguished American women. The length of the individual biographies varies with the importance of the woman and the availability of information concerning her. A brief bibliography of biographical sources and references follows each listing. Special features include a classified list of biographies by area in which the women distinguished themselves and an introduction briefly outlining the history of women in the United States.

34 Rutgers University. Center for the American Woman and Politics. Women in Public Office. N.Y.: R. R. Bowker, 1976.

Ref. HQ1391.U5 R8

Covers over 13,000 women active in politics on a national, state, and local level. Biographical section lists women by state, and within each state, by office. Includes name, address, office held, previous offices, party affiliations, organizational memberships, education, occupation, birthplace and date. An index by name of officeholder is provided. The data is current as of the first half of 1975. New editions are planned biennially to update the data. The statistical essay analyses the information on the women listed to determine if there are any discernible patterns which are characteristic of political women. Factors considered include number in office, individual background, family situation, organizational affiliations, and political experience and characteristics. The book provides a much-needed directory and a very revealing statistical survey.

35 Sosa de Newton, Lily.
Diccionario Biografico de Mujeres Argentinas. Buenos Aires, 1972.

Ref. Biog. CT3290.S67

A biographical dictionary, in Spanish, of prominent Argentinian women of the past and present.

36 Two Thousand Women of Achievement.
    Ed. by Ernest Kay. 3rd. ed. London: Melrose Press, 1971.
    Ref. Biog. CT3235.T94

    Brief biographies, listing personal details, career information, professional memberships, etc. Most entries include a photograph.

37 Ungherini, Aglauro.
    Manuel de Bibliographie Biographique et d'Iconographie des Femmes Célèbres. Turin: L. Roux, 1892.
    _____. Supplèment. Turin: Roux & Viarengo, 1900.
    _____. Second et dernier supplèment. Rome: Roux & Viarengo, 1905.   Ref. Z7963.B6 U5

    An index to material about women of all countries and all periods. An identifying phrase, dates of birth and death, monographic biographies in various languages, and locations of portraits, autographs, etc. are given. A cumulative index to the volumes is included in the second supplement.

38 U.S. Library of Congress. Division of Bibliography.
    List of References Relating to Notable American Women, compiled by F. S. Hellman. Washington, 1932, 1937, 1941.
    Ref. Z1229.W8 U5

    An index to material on women notable in various fields of activity from colonial times. There are three sections: a list of books on American women; an alphabetic list of notable women with references to citations to them in the books listed in the first section; and a selection of biographical dictionaries, encyclopedias, and books relating to women. There is a separate list for each of the years the list was published, a comprehensive author index for all three years, and a subject index.

39 U.S. Smithsonian Institution.
    Workers and Allies; female participation in the American trade union movement, 1824-1976, by Judith O'Sullivan and Rosemary Gallick. Washington, D.C.: Smithsonian Institution Press, 1975.   GPD SI1.2:W89/2

    Catalog of a photographic exhibition which also contains

much useful information. There is a chronology, pp. 25-32, short biographies of individual women with a bibliography for each, pp. 35-90, and a chronological bibliography of books, periodical articles and government publications, 1902-1975, pp. 91-96. There are no indexes.

40 Who's Who and Where in Women Studies.
Old Westbury, N.Y.: Feminist Press, 1974.
                                    Ref. Biog. HQ1181.U5 W48

A guide to feminist scholars and teachers, women's studies courses, and institutions which offer courses and programs. The list is divided into three sections, one by college, the second by name of faculty member, and the third lists courses by subject department.

41 Who's Who of American Women; a biographical dictionary of notable living American women.
Chicago: Marquis, 1958/59-   . v.1- . Current volume in
Ref. Biennial.   Ref. Biog. CT3260.W5

A biographical dictionary listing eminent women in current affairs. Included are all women in the latest edition of *Who's Who in America* and others chosen as most likely to be of reference interest because of position held or level of achievement. Information on education, personal life, career, and achievements is given.

42 Willard, Frances Elizabeth and Mary A. Livemore, eds.
A Woman of the Century, Fourteen Hundred-seventy Biographical Sketches Accompanied by Portraits of Leading American Women in All Walks of Life. Detroit: Gale Research Co., 1967. Reprint of Buffalo: C. W. Moulton, 1893.
                                    Ref. Biog. E176.W691 1967

This reprint edition of a 19th century biographical dictionary is a very useful source of information on women who made an impact on 19th century America. Many women listed do not appear in other biographical works. Portraits of the women are included with details on their lives and contributions.

43 Women's History Research Center, Inc.
Female Artists Past and Present. 2nd. ed. Berkeley, Calif., 1974.
                                    Ref. N43.W87 1974

Directory and bibliography of women's work in the visual arts. Individual women are listed alphabetically according to the media in which they work, with citations to writings on their work, mainly from women's movement publications. Addresses are given when known. There is a brief historical section on women artists and a section on the contemporary female artists' movement listing groups, galleries, publications, and exhibitions.

_____. Supplement, 1975.
Updates the second edition from April, 1974 on and includes a new section on Soviet artists and one on architecture.

FILMS AND FILMMAKERS

44 Betancourt, Jeanne.
  Women in Focus. Dayton, Ohio: Pflaum Publishing, 1974.
  Ref. PN1995.9.W6 B4

  Reviews non-sexist films, with an emphasis on those by women filmmakers. Includes biographical sketches on the filmmakers, a thematic index, a list of distributors, and a bibliography of related feminist readings.

45 Dawson, Bonnie.
  Women's Films in Print. San Francisco: Booklegger Press, 1975.   Ref. PN1998.D3

  Directory of the films of over 370 women filmmakers. 16mm films available for sale or rent are included. The directory is arranged by name of filmmaker, and film listings have brief descriptive annotations. There are indexes by subject and title, a distributors' address section, and a bibliography of works used in compiling the directory.

46 Smith, Sharon.
  Women Who Make Movies. N.Y.: Hopkinson and Blake, 1975.
  Ref. PN1998.A2 S57

  A history of women filmmakers in the U.S. and around the world, followed by an alphabetical directory of women filmmakers now working in the U.S. A list of organizations and film distributors is included. Name index.

ORGANIZATIONS

47 Barrer, Myra E., ed.
  Women's Organizations and Leaders, 1973- Directory. Washington: Today Publications and News Service, Inc.,

Current vol. in Ref. Biennial.   Ref. HQ1883.B37

Guide to more than 8,000 U.S. women's organizations and to individuals active in the women's movement. For each organization, national and local offices, leaders, activities, and goal statements are included. Listings for individuals include employment, group affiliations, and publications. There are three indexes: an alphabetical list of organizations and individuals; a geographical listing of organizations and individuals by state; and a subject index of organizations and individuals by their area of interest.

48   Harrison, Cynthia.
     Women's Movement Media; a source guide. N.Y.: Bowker, 1975.
     Ref. Z7964.U49 H37

     A multi-media resource guide to groups serving women's interests. The directory includes publishers and producers of media, women's research centers and libraries, women's organizations, government agencies, and groups serving special interests within the women's movement. Each entry gives the organization's title, address, contact person, purpose, and available items. Four indexes make the directory very useful: a geographic index of groups; a title index of available media; an index of groups by name; and a subject index of groups.

49   Human Rights Organizations and Periodicals Directory.
     Berkeley, Calif.: Meiklejohn Civil Liberties Institute, 1975.
     Ref. KF4741.H84 1975

     Directory of mainly national organizations concerned with the legal aspects of human rights, and of human rights journals. The directory is divided into an alphabetical list of organizations and serials and a subject index. Listings are annotated. Subject headings used include: abortion; discrimination—sex; women.

50   Johnson, Willis.
     Directory of Special Programs for Minority Group Members: Career Information Services, Employment Skills Banks, Financial Aid Services. 2nd. ed. Garret Park, Md.: Garret Park Press, 1975.   Ref. L901.J64 1975

Section 3 lists women's programs with addresses and brief descriptions.

51 National Council of Women of the United States.
International Directory of Women's Organizations. N.Y.: Research and Action Association, 1963.

Ref. HQ1883.N3

This directory, though dated, gives valuable information on international and U.S. women's organizations, including purpose, date of founding, membership, affiliations, officers, and address. It is arranged in six groupings by type of organization. No index.

STATISTICS

52 American Statistics Index.
    1974 Annual and Retrospective Edition, First Annual
    Supplement 1975, 1976- . Washington, D.C.: Congressional
    Information Service, 1974- . GPD RR

    "A comprehensive guide and index to the statistical
    publications of the U.S. government." Indexes every table in
    statistical publications, and individual tables in other items.
    Most useful indexing is under subject "women," headings
    beginning with "women's," and "by sex" in Index by
    Categories. Monthly abstracts and indexes, six month index
    cumulations, yearly cumulations of abstracts and indexes.

53 Canada. Dominion Bureau of Statistics, Census Division.
    The Female Worker in Canada, by Sylvia Ostry. Ottawa,
    Ontario: Queen's Printer, 1968. (1961 Census Monograph:
    Special Labor Force Study)   GPD Can1-S2.11:F34

    Discussion of statistical results of the 1961 census of Canada,
    showing the place of women in working life. Some
    comparisons to earlier data also shown.

54 Canada. Women's Bureau.
    Women in the Labour Force: Facts and Figures. 1975 edition.
    Ottawa: Information Canada, 1975.
                                    GPD Can1-L4.6:975

    Statistical data on Canadian women in the labor force. One
    section deals specifically with working mothers. Some figures
    from the 1971 census are included, but most are from 1974.

55 Great Britain. Department of Employment.

Women and Work: a Statistical Survey. London: HMSO, 1974. (Manpower Paper, no. 9)   **GPD GtB1-ER1.6:9**

Compilation of statistics from various official sources about women and work. Sections covered include: economic activity; numbers in employment; women not at work; occupations; and employment behavior. Most figures are for 1971, with some comparisons to earlier years.

56 Russia (USSR, 1923-). Tsentral'noe Statisticheskoe Upravlenie. Zhenshchiny i Deti v SSSR: Statisticheskii Sbornik. Moscow, 1960- .   **GPD RUS2-S1.12:year**

Statistics on the status of women and children in Russia to show that equality of the sexes exists. The library currently owns issues for 1960, 1961, and 1963 which contain some statistics back to the 1930's for comparative purposes.

57 _____.

Zhenshchiny v SSSR: Statisticheskii Sbornik. Moscow, n.d.
                    GPD RUS2-S1.2:Z6

Statistical compilation on women in the USSR. Includes historical data.

58 U.S. Census Bureau.
A Statistical Portrait of Women in the United States. Washington, D.C.: U.S.G.P.O., 1976. (Current Population reports: Special Studies: Series P-23, no. 58)
                    GPD C3.186:P-23/58

More than 75 tables in 14 subject areas. Statistics are based on sample counts with separate chapters on Black and Spanish women. Contains a larger number and variety of statistics than the *Handbook on Women Workers*, but no textual information.

59 _____.

Statistics of Women at Work Based on Unpublished Information Derived from the Schedules of the Twelfth Census: 1900. Washington, D.C.: U.S.G.P.O., 1907. (Special Report of the Census Office) **GPD C3.5:W84**

Based on the original census questionnaires, this report gives a detailed statistical picture of the types of labor being performed, and other data for women at the turn of the century. Also contains some comparisons with earlier census reports.

60 ————.

Women-owned Businesses, 1972. Washington, D.C.:
U.S.G.P.O., 1976.   GPD C3.250:72

Statistical compendium from the 1972 economic census
program on businesses owned by women. Statistics also on
minority businesses owned by women. Report indicates most
businesses owned by women were in retail trade and services.

61 U.S. Labor Statistics Bureau.

U.S. Working Women; a chartbook. Washington, D.C.:
U.S.G.P.O., 1975. 56 Charts. (BLS Bulletin, no. 1880)
GPD L2.3:1880

Statistical data presented in chart form only. The latest data
date from 1974. Sources are given to help in updating the
statistics. Most useful for graphic presentations.

INDEXES, ABSTRACTS, AND BIBLIOGRAPHIES

WOMEN'S STUDIES

62 Barnard College, N.Y. Women's Center.
Women's Work and Women's Studies, 1971- . Pittsburgh: Know, Inc., 1972- . Annual. Ref. Z7961.B33

Summary of the year's scholarship in women's studies, including many dissertations and works in progress. Items are arranged by broad subject areas and most are annotated. Author index.

63 Canada (Quebec). Bibliotheque Nationale du Quebec.
La Femme au Quebec, by Ghislaine Houle. Montreal: Bibliotheque Nationale du Quebec, Ministere des Affairs Culturelles, 1975. (Bibliographies Quebeçoises, no. 1)
GPD Can10-AC2.7:1

Unannotated list of books, periodical articles, and Canadian government publications, all in French, published from the late 1960's to 1974. Listings are by author in the following general classes: political and legal situation; women and labor; sexuality; consciousness raising; literature; and biographies. Author and title indexes.

64 Cardinale, Susan.
Special Issues of Serials about Women, 1965-1975. Monticello, Ill., 1976. (Council of Planning Librarians Exchange Bibliography, no. 995) Ref. Z5942.C68 no. 995

Annotated list of issues of periodicals devoted to the subject of women. Arranged alphabetically by periodical title. Includes both special sections of issues and those entirely devoted to women.

65 Davis, Audrey B.
Bibliography on Women. N.Y.: Science History Publications, 1974. Ref. Z7405.P7 D36

Pamphlet listing books and articles on women's roles in science and society. Arranged alphabetically.

66 Davis, Lenwood G.
The Black Woman in American Society; a selected annotated bibliography. Boston: G. K. Hall, 1975.
Ref. Z1361.N39 D36

Reference book on the life and achievements of U.S. black women from earliest times to the present. Indexed material includes books, articles, current black periodicals, reports, pamphlets, speeches, and government documents. Also included: lists of U.S. libraries with black history collections; national organizations of black women; black women newspaper publishers, editors, and elected officials; and statistics on black women in rural and urban areas. Indexed by subject and author.

67 _____.

The Woman in American Society; a selected bibliography. Monticello, Ill., 1974. (Council of Planning Librarians Exchange Bibliography, no. 554)
Ref. Z5942.C68 no. 554

Very general list of books on women in the U.S. A list of selected women's periodicals also included.

_____. _____.

2nd ed. Monticello, Ill., 1975. (Council of Planning Librarians Exchange Bibliography, no. 810-811)
Ref. Z5942.C68 no. 810-811

Books, women's periodicals, government publications, biographical works, women's organizations, and women college presidents are listed in this second edition. No index.

68 Knight, Mary Jane and Susan Sturgeon.
Feminist Library and Women's Center. Honolulu: Graduate School of Library Studies, University of Hawaii, 1974.
Ref. Dept.

Unpublished bibliography of books recommended for beginning a women's center library. The bibliography is on 3" by 5" cards and is arranged by subject.

69 Kratochvil, Laura and Shauna Shaw.
    African Women; a select bibliography. Cambridge: African
    Studies Centre, 1974.   Ref. Z7964.A3 K7

    Selected bibliography of periodicals, books, theses, official
    publications, conference proceedings, and unpublished
    material on African women in English and several European
    languages. Subject arrangement with regional and author
    indexes. Useful for researching the status of women in
    developing African countries.

70 Krichmar, Albert.
    The Women's Rights Movement in the United States,
    1848-1970; a bibliography and sourcebook. Metuchen, N.J.:
    Scarecrow Press, 1972.   Ref. Z7964.U49 K75

    Covers legal and political status of women; equal rights
    amendment; suffrage; economic status; women in law,
    medicine, business, politics, science, education, and religion.
    Organized by subject, with author, subject, and manuscript
    index. Manuscript collections, women's liberation periodicals,
    and a biographical section are also included.

71 Rosenberg, Marie Barovic and Len V. Bergstrom.
    Women and Society. Beverly Hills, Calif.: Sage Publications,
    1975.   Ref. Z7961.A67

    Selected, briefly annotated bibliography of the scholarship
    and research on women in many disciplines, e.g., sociology,
    political science, history, psychology, etc. Books, journal
    articles, and pamphlets are included, arranged in an extensive
    subject breakdown, e.g., women in folklore and witchcraft
    under history, or women in domestic labor under economics.
    There is an author/organization index, index of journal issues
    devoted to women, index of persons not cited as authors, and
    index of places, subjects, and topics.

72 Rowbotham, Sheila.
    Women's Liberation and Revolution. 2nd ed. Montpelier,
    Bristol, England: Falling Water Press, 1973.
                                   Ref. Z7961.R67 1973

    Briefly annotated list of pamphlets, articles, and books on the
    relationship between feminism and revolutionary politics.
    Arranged by subject and covers such areas as the effect of
    capitalism on women at work and in the home, the changing

nature of the family, women and the socialist movement, the connection between culture, consciousness, and revolutionary change, etc.

73 South Dakota. Commission on the Status of Women.
    South Dakota Women 1850-1919; a bibliography. Pierre, South Dakota: Commission on the Status of Women, 1975.
    GPD 41-W84.2:W84

    Short list of bibliographies, then longer lists of fiction and non-fiction entries. Publication dates for the books and pamphlets range from the 1800's to the present. Short annotations give some idea of the content. Locations in at least one library are also given.

74 United Nations. Dag Hammarskjold Library.
    Status of Women; a select bibliography. New York: United Nations, 1975. (Bibliographical Series, no. 20)
    GPD UN-ST/LIB/Ser.B/20

    Lists major books, articles, and government publications of the past ten years. Organized by subject, then continent, then individual country. No indexes.

75 U.S. Housing and Urban Development Department.
    "Equal Opportunity for Women in Housing; a bibliography" in: *Women and Housing; a report on sex discrimination in five American cities.* Washington, D.C.: U.S.G.P.O., 1975, pp. 175-196.   GPD HH1.2:W84/3

    Covers books, periodical and newspaper articles, and government publications for the period 1970-1974. Arranged by subject with author index.

76 Williams, Ora.
    American Black Women in the Arts and Social Sciences; a bibliographic survey. Metuchen, N.J.: Scarecrow Press, 1973.
    Ref. Z1361.N39 W56 1973

    Includes writings and audio-visual materials with a section on the works of fifteen individual women. Name index.

77 Women Studies Abstracts.
    Ed. by Sara Stauffer Whaley. Rush, N.Y., Winter, 1972- .
    v.1- . Quarterly.   Ref. Dept.

    Indexes material of interest in women's studies from a wide range of academic disciplines. Useful as a current awareness tool for new research and programs. Subject areas covered include art, education, employment, family, health, history, literature, sex roles, and the women's movement. Book reviews and feature articles on topics such as women's films, women in politics, and sex stereotypes in children's books are included. About two hundred abstracts appear in each issue, in a classified subject arrangement with author and subject indexes; indexes are cumulated annually.

78 Pamphlet bibliographies and other pamphlets of current interest may be found in the Reference Department's pamphlet and bibliography files. Sources of these materials include private organizations, libraries, foundations, etc. The files are arranged by subject and topics covered include single parents; women— education; women—employment; women—self-defense, etc.

Bibliographies on Individual Women

In addition to bibliographies of material on women as a group, there are numerous bibliographies on the works and contributions of individual women. Some of these are listings of a woman's writings and descriptions of the various editions of her writings; others include critical material on the woman's works or writings about her. To find a bibliography on a person, look in the subject half of the card catalog under the individual's name, with the subdivision "bibliography." Any book-length bibliographies on the person will be listed. Bibliographies which appear in journal articles or as sections of books can be located by using the *Bibliographic Index*. Some examples of the various types of bibliographies on individuals follow.

79 AUSTEN, JANE
    Roth, Barry and Joel Weinsheimer.
        An Annotated Bibliography of Jane Austen Studies 1952-1972.
        Charlottesville: University Press of Virginia, 1973.
                                    Ref. Z8048.R65

    Annotated bibliography of critical books, essays, articles, and dissertations; indexed by author and subject.

80 BRONTË FAMILY
    Wise, Thomas James.
        A Bibliography of the Writings in Prose and Verse of the Members of the Brontë Family. London: Dawsons of Pall Mall, 1965. Reprint of 1917 ed., London: R. Clay and Sons.
                                    Ref. Z8122.W68

Descriptive bibliography; also lists complete volumes of biography and criticism published before 1917.

81 MARIE ANTOINETTE
Tourneux, Maurice.
Marie-Antoinette devant l'Histoire. 2nd ed., rev. Paris: H. Leclerc, 1901.   Ref. Z8550.3.T7

82 O'CONNOR, FLANNERY
Dorsey, J. E. "Carson McCullers and Flannery O'Connor: a Checklist of Graduate Research." *Bulletin of Bibliography*, 32 (October 1975): 162-167.

83 PLATH, SYLVIA
Northouse, Cameron and Thomas P. Walsh.
Sylvia Plath and Anne Sexton; a reference guide. Boston: G. K. Hall and Co., 1974.   Ref. Z8695.85.N67

Divided into two sections, one for each poet. Lists works and major criticisms chronologically. Criticisms are annotated. Separate indexes for each section.

84 WOOLF, VIRGINIA
Kirkpatrick, Brownlee Jean.
A Bibliography of virginia Woolf. Rev. ed. London: Rupert Hart-Davis, 1967.   Ref. Z8984.2.K5 1967

Lists her writings, including letters and manuscripts. Indexed.

RELATED FIELDS

Anthropology

85 Abstracts in Anthropology.
Westport, Ct.: Greenwood Periodicals, 1970- . v.1- . Quarterly.   Ref. Dept.

Classified arrangement by field: archaeology; cultural anthropology; linguistics; and physical anthropology. Author and subject index are included in each issue. Subject index terms include sex differences, sex roles, and women's studies. Books, articles, and conference papers are indexed, with a list of journals abstracted at the end of each issue. Coverage international, but English language materials predominate. Cultural anthropology section is of most interest in women's studies, including a section on family organization and marriage under "kinship," and a section on male-female relations under "minorities."

86 Current Bibliography on African Affairs.
     Washington, D.C.: African Bibliographic Center, 1968- . n.s.
     v.1- . Quarterly.   Ref. Z3501.C85

Selected list of scholarly books, government documents, and periodical articles. Feature articles, book reviews, bibliographical section arranged by subject and region, and author index are included. Items on African women are included in the general subject category of the bibliographic section.

87 Human Relations Area Files, Inc.
     HRAF Microfiles. New Haven. 196- . (Microfiche)
                                        Micro/Media Dept.

The HRAF Microfiles are a collection of ethnographic data on many primitive and non-primitive societies. Sources "processed" for the files include books, articles, and manuscripts, mostly reports of original field work done by anthropologists (see *HRAF Source Bibliography.* New Haven, 1969- . Ref. Z7161.H82). The collection is indexed by the following sources:

Murdock, George Peter. Outline of World Cultures. 4th ed. rev. New Haven, 1972. (Behavior Science Outlines v. 3)
                              Ref. H62.B36 v.3 1972

Index to the cultures and societies covered from each country; the table of contents lists countries within each continent, while the index at the end lists individual groups of people, e.g., Iroquois, Somali, etc. An alphanumeric code is given for each culture.

_____. Outline of Cultural Materials. 4th rev. ed. New Haven, 1971. (Behavior Science Outlines v. 1)
                              Ref. H62.B36 v.1 1971

Explanation and index to the subject breakdown of the collection; subject areas of interest: 462 Labor—division of labor by sex; 562 Social stratification—sex status; 58 Marriage; 59 Family; 60 Kinship; 61 Kin groups; 684 Offenses and sanctions—sex and marital offenses; 83 Sex; 84 Reproduction; 85 Infancy and childhood; 86 Socialization. By pairing the code for a culture with the subject number, one can retrieve materials from the files on a given culture which deal with a specific topic.

88 International Bibliography of Social and Cultural Anthropology.
    London: Tavistock; Chicago: Aldine, 1955- . v.1- . Annual.
                         Ref. Z7161.I593

    Selected list of over four thousand books and articles per year;
    classified arrangement with author and subject indexes in
    English and French. Useful subject terms include: family;
    fertility; girls; marriage; puberty rites; women. Publication lag
    is approximately two years.

89 Jacobs, Sue-Ellen.
    Women in Perspective; a guide for cross-cultural studies.
    Urbana: University of Illinois Press, 1974.
                         Ref. Z7961.J3

    Compilation of brief, informative bibliographies on women
    in various cultures and on topics relevant to women. Part I has
    a geographical arrangement of items dealing with women in
    various countries from ancient to modern times. Part II
    consists of bibliographies on a wide range of topics: women
    and religion; prostitution; women in prison; political roles;
    women in history; women in literature, etc. Provides an
    excellent beginning point for student research in many areas
    of women's studies.

Art and Architecture

90 Art Index.
    N.Y.: H. W. Wilson, 1933- . v.1- . Quarterly, cumulated
    annually.   Ref. Dept.

    Author and subject index to a selected list of U.S. and foreign
    fine arts periodicals in the fields of archaeology, architecture,
    art history, arts and crafts, films, fine arts, graphic arts,
    industrial design, interior decoration, landscaping, and
    photography. Useful terms include: models, artist's;
    photography of women; women; women as architects, artists,
    etc.; women in art; women in moving pictures; women's
    liberation movement.

91 Johnson, Carolyn R.
    Women in Architecture; an annotated bibliography and guide
    to sources of information. Monticello, Ill., 1974. (Council of
    Planning Librarians Exchange Bibliography, no. 549)
                         Ref. Z5942.C68 no. 549

Books and periodical articles concerning architectural career opportunities for women, achievements of women architects, organizations of women in architecture, and statistical sources on women in architecture. Subject arrangement.

92 Worldwide Art Catalogue Bulletin.
Boston, Mass.: Worldwide Book Inc., 1964- . v.1- . Quarterly.   Ref. Z5937.W67

Annotated listing of catalogues arranged by country. Title, artist, chronological, media, and topical indexes are included. "Women artists" is used as an index term in the topical index.

Business and Economics

93 American Economic Association.
Index of Economic Articles in Journals and Collective Volumes. 1886- . Homewood, Ill.: Irwin, 1961- . Annual.
Ref. Dept.

Arrangement is by a detailed classification system with author index and a topical index to the classification schedule at the end of the volume. There is also a list of journals and books indexed. Topical indexing under: household, economics of; woman labor, wages of; women—as demographic components in labor force; women—discrimination.

94 Business Periodicals Index.
N.Y.: H. W. Wilson, 1958- . v.1- . Monthly (except July), cumulated annually.   Ref. Dept.

Subject index to English language periodicals in the business field. Successor to the business portion of the *Industrial Arts Index*, 1913-1957. Headings concerning women include: advertising—women, appeal to; education of women; mothers; prostitution; widows; wives; women (with subdivisions); women as . . .; women in . . .; women's liberation movement.

95 Funk and Scott Index of Corporations and Industries.
Cleveland, Ohio: Predicasts, 1970- . v.1- . Weekly, cumulated monthly and annually.
Ref. Dept.

Index to over 750 periodicals and other materials such as company reports. Emphasizes activities of U.S. companies and industries, in contrast to *Business Periodicals Index,* which covers more general business factors. Divided into two sections, one covering general economic factors, and one dealing with individual companies. Section one is arranged by SIC (Standard Industrial Classification), a numerical code which groups related products and factors. There is a guide to the SIC's given, and women's liberation has been assigned SIC number, 865 6100. The researcher can find material on general economic trends affecting women in section one or research a specific company involved with women, such as in a fair employment practice case, by looking under the company's name in section two.

96   International Bibliography of Economics.
       London: Tavistock; Chicago: Aldine, 1952- . v.1- . Annual.
                                                 Ref. Dept.

       Extensive, classified list of books, articles, and reports in many languages. Author and subject indexes and a list of periodicals indexed are given. "Employment, women" is the significant topic covered.

97   Journal of Economic Literature.
       Nashville: American Economic Association, 1963- . v.1- .
       Quarterly.   Ref. Dept.

       Formerly *Journal of Economic Abstracts,* 1963-1968, v. 1-6; an abstracting index, arranged by journal, with a subject index in each issue and annual author index. With March, 1969, the journal became a literature reviewing source divided into several sections: feature articles; communications; book reviews; new books; and current periodicals. The periodicals section consists of a current contents section listing tables of contents of over two hundred current economics journals, a classified subject index to these articles and selected abstracts of some. There is a yearly cumulated author index of authors of articles, review articles, book reviews, communications, and abstracts. Items on women and economics may be found in sections 800 (manpower, labor, population) and 900 (welfare programs, consumer economics, urban and regional economics).

98   World Agricultural Economics and Rural Sociology Abstracts.
       Farnham Royal, Bucks, England: Commonwealth Agricultural Bureaux, 1959- . v.1- . Monthly.
                                                 Ref. Dept.

International bibliography on agricultural policy, legislation, agrarian reform, international trade, geography, history, and agrarian education as they relate to agricultural economy and rural sociology. Classified arrangement with cumulative author, subject, and geographic indexes. Useful for information on rural women in foreign countries. Index terms include female labour, housewives, women.

Education

99   Astin, Helen S.
     Women; a bibliography on their education and careers. N.Y.: Behavioral Publications, Inc., 1974.
                                    Ref. Z7963.E7 A86 1974

     Abstracts of 350 studies conducted between 1960 and 1970 arranged into sections on determining career choice, continuing education, marital and family status of working women, women in the world of work, etc. Indexed by subject and author.

100 British Education Index.
     London: Library Association, 1954- . v.1- . Three times a year, cumulated annually.   Ref. Dept.

     Index, by subject and author, to about 150 selected British periodicals and some conference papers. Subject terms used include women (with subdivisions); women, study of; women and girls: education.

101 College Student Personnel Abstracts.
     Claremont, Calif.: College Student Personnel Institute, 1969 . v.5- . Quarterly.   Ref. Dept.

     Covers over one hundred journals, conference proceedings, books, and research reports pertaining to college students and college student services. Arrangement by topic with author and subject indexing. Birth control, marriage, pregnancy, sex, women, and women's studies are relevant subject indexing terms.

102 Current Index to Journals in Education.
     N.Y.: CCM Information Corp., 1969- . v.1- . Monthly.
                                    Ref. Dept.

     Indexes over 700 education and education-related periodicals. Annotated references are followed by subject, author, and journal contents indexes. Useful index terms: unwed mothers; women professors; women teachers; women's athletics; women's education; women's studies. *CIJE* is a cooperative effort between the ERIC (Educational Resources Information Center) program and the Crowell, Collier and Macmillan Information Corporation.

103 Education Index.
N.Y.: H. W. Wilson, 1929- . v.1- . Monthly (except July and August), cumulated annually.

Ref. Dept.

Author and subject index to English language educational material in about 250 periodicals, proceedings of conferences, yearbooks, and bulletins. Prior to 1961, books, government documents and reports were indexed also. Author entries deleted from 1962-1969 were reinstated in 1970. Pertinent subject entries include: athletics for girls and women; business and professional women; college students, women; femininity; married women; Negro women; teachers, married women; women (with subdivisions).

104 International Bureau of Education.
Education and Training of Women, prepared by Françoise Cismaresco. Paris: Unesco, 1975. (Educational Documentation and Information Bulletin no. 196).

GPD IBE-3:196

Lists books, periodical articles, and government documents published between 1970 and 1975. There is a section of general works with remaining items arranged geographically. Updates Bulletin no. 174, 1970.

105 International Reading Association.
IRA Annotated Bibliography: Sex Differences and Reading. comp. by E. Marcia Sheridan. Newark, Del.: International Reading Association, 1976.   Ref. Z5814.R25 I5 no. 27

Includes studies of sex differences based on reading methods, sex of teacher, separate sex classes, treatment of boys and girls, etc. Also lists some background materials on sex role development.

106 Resources in Education.
U.S. Educational Resources Information Center (ERIC) Washington, D.C.: U.S.G.P.O., Nov., 1966- . v.1- . Monthly.   Ref. Dept.

Annotated bibliography announcing recently completed reports of federally funded research projects, conference proceedings, bibliographies, and professional papers in the field of education. Subject, author, and institution indexes are presently cumulated twice a year. The Educational Resources Information Center is part of the U.S. Dept. of Health, Education and Welfare and is responsible for maintaining a nationwide network for acquiring, abstracting, and disseminating "significant and timely education-related reports." Most documents are available on microfiche; access is by the ED number assigned to each document in the bibliography. Pertinent subject terms include: females, sex discrimination; women; women's education; women's studies; working women. Consult the *Thesaurus of ERIC Descriptors*, shelved with the index, for additional search terms.

107 Westervelt, Esther Manning, et. al.
Women's Higher and Continuing Education. N.Y.: College Entrance Examination Board, 1971.
Ref. Z7963.E2 W43

Annotated bibliography with major emphasis on women's education in the U.S. and secondary emphasis on material pertaining to women's employment and more general matters. Books, journal articles, government publications, and conference proceedings are included. Arrangement is topical, with most items cited dating from the 1960's.

108 Yearbook of Equal Educational Opportunity 1975-76- .
Chicago: Marquis Academic Media, 1975- .
Ref. LA201.Y43

Includes government and private agency statistics and reports on education-related problems involving various groups. Part five, "Women," reviews current legislation and includes comparative material on the status of women and men in education. Most of the materials are reprints from government documents. Subject index.

Employment

109 Bickner, Mei Liang.
Women at Work; an annotated bibliography. Los Angeles: Manpower Research Center, Institute of Industrial Relations, University of California, 1974. Ref. Z7963.E7 B5

A bibliography of research studies and articles on working women, most dating after 1960. Emphasis is on legal developments affecting working women, women in the labor movement, and non-professional and minority women. Arrangement is by subject, with author, title, keyword, and category indexes.

110   BNA Looseleaf Services:
Washington, D.C.: Bureau of National Affairs.

Fair Employment Practice Cases. 1969- . v.1- .
Ref. HD4903.F35

Labor Arbitration Reports. 1946- . v.1- .
Ref. HD5487.U5 L3

Labor Relations Reference Manual. 1935- . v.1- .
Ref. HD5503.A7224

Wage and Hour Cases, 1939- . v.1- .
Ref. HD4974.W3

Detailed and highly complex arrangement of materials on the law of labor relations. Includes new developments, laws and executive orders, court opinions, and decisions of the National Labor Relations Board. The master index volume should be consulted first, where a how to use section will be found. Useful for information on sex discrimination cases.

111   Business and Professional Women's Foundation.
Women Executives; a selected annotated bibliography. Washington, 1970.   Ref. Z7963.E7 B79 1970

The foundation's purpose is to conduct and support research on the economic, social, and psychological challenges confronting women. This bibliography concentrates on material published mainly between 1960 and 1970, ranging from the popular to the scholarly level. Books, pamphlets, reports, periodical articles, theses, and microfilm are included. Arrangement is alphabetical by author.

112   Hughes, Marija Matich.
The Sexual Barrier; legal and economic aspects of employment. San Francisco, 1970.
———— Supplement 1-2, 1971-72. 2v.
Ref. Z7963.E7 H8

Subjects treated include discrimination in hiring and promotion, pay differences, educational barriers to women, employment of women in foreign countries, and the equal rights amendment. Materials listed date mainly from 1959 and include books, periodical articles, pamphlets, and government documents.

113 International Labour Office.
Bibliography on Women Workers, 1861-1965. Geneva: International Labour Office, 1970. (Bibliographical Contributions, no. 26)   **GPD ILO-24:26**

Includes books, periodical articles, and government publications in many languages. Basic arrangement by broad subject headings, then chronological. Indexing by personal and corporate author, subject, and geographical area.

114 Ohio. State University, Columbus. Center for Vocational and Technical Education.
Implications of Women's Work Patterns for Vocational and Technical Education; an annotated bibliography. Columbus, 1967.   **Ref. Z5814.T4 04 no. 1**

Annotated bibliography of books, government publications, and journal articles dating primarily between 1964 and 1967. Divided into several sections: status of women; education of women for employment; labor force participation of women; legislation pertaining to women in the labor force; vocational guidance research; bibliographies; and presentations appropriate for students.

115 Personnel Management Abstracts.
Ann Arbor, Mich.: Bureau of Industrial Relations, Graduate School of Business Administration, University of Michigan, 1968- . v.14- . Quarterly.   **Ref. Dept.**

Covers books and articles from academic and trade journals dealing with the management of people and organizational behavior. Arranged by subject, with author and title indexes. Includes separate abstract section where selected entries are abstracted. Equal opportunity is a useful subject search term.

116 Sharma, Prakash C.
Female Working Role and Economic Development; a selected research bibliography. Monticello, Ill., 1974. (Council of Planning Librarians Exchange Bibliography, no. 663)
Ref. Z5942.C68 no. 663

International bibliography on working women, including

books and periodical articles from 1940-1972, arranged alphabetically by author.

117 Soltow, Martha and Mary K. Wery.
American Women and the Labor Movement, 1825-1974; an annotated bibliography. Metuchen, N.J.: Scarecrow Pr., 1976.
Ref. Z7963.E7 S635 1976

Bibliography on women's general work conditions, unions, strikes, protective legislation, and labor leaders. Books, journal articles, pamphlets, and government publications are cited. Contains author and subject index with appendix listing U.S. archives of material relating to women and labor.

118 U.S. Civil Service Commission.
"Employment of Women—Selected Books and Articles" in: *Equal Opportunity in Employment*. Washington, D.C.: U.S.G.P.O., 1973, pp. 132-170. (Personnel Bibliography, no. 49)
GPD CS1.61/3:49

Short annotations of books, periodical articles, and government publications published from 1971-73. Entries are arranged alphabetically by author in three sections: a general bibliography; executive, managerial and professional opportunities; and women in the federal government. No indexes. Updates similar material in Personnel Bibliography no. 38, 1971.

119 U.S. Equal Employment Opportunity Commission.
"Annotated Bibliography" in: *Affirmative Actions Programs for Women; a survey of innovative programs*. Washington, D.C.: U.S.G.P.O., 1973, pp. 119-150.
GPD Y3.Eq2:2W84/2

Divided into sections on specific topics such as "Women's place in society," "Women and labor unions," "The legal point of view." Within each section arrangement is by author. Covers books, periodical articles, and government publications published from 1960-1972. No index.

120 U.S. Women's Bureau.
Employment of Older Women; an annotated bibliography. Washington, D.C.: U.S.G.P.O., 1957.
GPD L13.2:011/5-957

Lengthy annotations of books, periodical articles, and

government publications in the areas of hiring practices, attitudes, and work performance. Alphabetical by author, with subject index; covers approximately 1950-1956.

General

BIBLIOGRAPHIC INDEXES

121 Besterman, Theodore.
      A World Bibliography of Bibliographies. 4th ed. Laussane: Societas Bibliographica, 1965-1966. 5v.

            Ref. Z1001.B5686

      Alphabetical listing by subject of over 100,000 bibliographies published through 1963. Brief annotations are given, with estimate of the number of items in each bibliography. Volume five is an index of authors, editors, translators, titles of serials, and anonymous works, libraries, and archives. The subject heading "women" is divided into five sections: general; countries; education; suffrage; and miscellaneous. Erotica, gynecology, and vocational guidance—women are also used as subject headings.

122 Bibliographic Index.
      N.Y.: H. W. Wilson, 1937- . v.1- . Three issues a year.

            Ref. Z1002.B594

      Excellent subject listing of bibliographies of more than fifty items which appear in books, periodicals, and pamphlets. Many listings appear under the heading "women" and related terms, e.g., authors, women; education of women; women as poets and the names of individual women.

123 Bulletin of Bibliography.
      Boston: F. W. Faxon, 1897- . v.1- . Quarterly.

            Ref. Z1007.B94

      Publishes bibliographies on a wide range of topics in the humanities and social sciences. Indexed by *Bibliographic Index*. One useful article, for example:

      Rothstein, Pauline Marcus. "Books on Women." *Bulletin of Bibliography* 32 (April-June 1975): 45-54, 76.

BOOK REVIEWS

124   Book Review Digest.
        N.Y.: H. W. Wilson. 1905- . v.1- . Monthly, cumulated
        annually.   Ref. Dept.

        Book reviews of general English language materials with brief
        descriptive notes on the book's content, quotes from several
        reviews, and brief bibliography of other reviews. Length of
        reviews is indicated. Author approach, supplemented by title
        and subject indexes which cumulate every five years. Useful
        for critical evaluation of a modern woman author, or to find
        reviews of books on women by using the subject index.

125   Book Review Index.
        Detroit: Gale Research, 1965- . v.1- . Quarterly, cumulated
        annually.   Ref. Dept.

        Cites book reviews, by author, in about 225 North American
        and British newspapers, general magazines, and journals.
        Especially strong in the social sciences. Unlike *Book Review
        Digest*, no quotations from reviews are given, but more books
        are covered. Author approach only.

126   Current Book Review Citations.
        N.Y.: H. W. Wilson, 1976- . v.1- . Monthly (except
        August).   Ref. Dept.

        Indexes reviews in over 1,000 periodicals. Includes reviews
        indexed in all other Wilson Co. indexes. Arrangement by
        author with title index.

127   New York Times Book Review Index 1896-1970.
        N.Y.: New York Times and Arno Press, 1973. 5v.
                                               Ref. Dept.

        Index to all material appearing in the Sunday *New York
        Times* book review section with the exception of
        advertisements and questions to the editor. Approach is by
        author, title, byline, subject, or category (literary genre).
        Entries for items other than book reviews include a brief
        summary of the item itself. Citations are to date and page
        number. Book reviews in weekday issues of the *New York
        Times* are not included. Useful for an author search and also
        for a subject search under the heading "women," which is
        subdivided by country, and for the United States, further
        subdivided by chronological period.

DISSERTATIONS

128 U.S. Library of Congress. Catalog Division.
List of American Doctoral Dissertations Printed in 1912-38.
Washington, D.C.: U.S.G.P.O., 1913-1940.
Ref. Z5055.U49 U5

Lists only printed dissertations.

129 Doctoral Dissertations Accepted by American Universities, 1933/34-1954/55.
Compiled for the Association of Research Libraries. New York: H. W. Wilson, 1934-56. Ref. Z5055.V49 D6

Continued by:

130 Index to American Doctoral Dissertations, 1955/56-1962/63.
Compiled for the Association of Research Libraries. Ann Arbor, Mich.: University Microfilms, 1957-64.
Ref. Z5055.U49 A5

Changed title to:

131 American Doctoral Dissertations, 1963/64- .
Compiled for the Association of Research Libraries. Ann Arbor, Mich.: University Microfilms, 1965- . Annual.
Ref. Z5055.U49 A5

Lists all dissertations accepted by universities in the United States. Broad subject arrangement, with author indexes.

132 Dissertation Abstracts International; abstracts of dissertations available on microfilm or as xerographic reproductions (formerly Dissertation Abstracts).
Ann Arbor, Mich.: University Microfilms, 1938- . v.1- .
Monthly. Ref. Z5055.U5 A53

Contains lengthy abstracts of doctoral dissertations submitted to University Microfilms by more than 270 institutions. Most major American universities co-operate, as well as some Canadian and European schools. Dissertations are microfilmed and are available for purchase from the company. Arrangement by subject with author and keyword title indexes. Since 1966, there have been two separate sections, A (humanities and social sciences) and B (sciences and engineering).

133 Comprehensive Dissertation Index, 1861-1972.

Ann Arbor, Mich.: Xerox University Microfilms, 1973. 37v.
────. Supplement. 1973- . Ann Arbor, 1974- . Annual.
Ref. Z5053.X47

An attempt to list all doctoral dissertations accepted in the United States up to 1972, with annual supplements covering later years. Some foreign dissertations are also listed. Serves as an index to all of the above lists of dissertations, plus listings of dissertations from many schools not otherwise covered. Arrangement by subject, with author index. Entries are listed under keywords from dissertation titles, within broad subject volumes. A search can be made for dissertations on women in education, for example, by checking the volume on education under women and appropriate related terms.

134   Masters Abstracts.
Ann Arbor, Mich.: Xerox University Microfilms, 1962- .
v.1- . Quarterly.   Ref. Dept.

Catalog of masters theses which are on microfilm and available for purchase from Xerox University Microfilms. Arranged by subject with author and subject indexes which cumulate annually and every five years. Co-operating institutions are listed. Sociology—family, Psychology—social, and Health sciences—nursing are among useful search terms.

135   In addition to the above, the Reference Department maintains a card file which lists bibliographies of theses and dissertations, both U.S. and foreign, in various subject fields.

GENERAL PERIODICAL INDEXES

136   Alternative Press Index.
Baltimore, Md.: Alternative Press Center, Inc., 1969- . v.1-3, 6- . (Publication of v.4-5, 1972-73, has been postponed).
Spec. Ref. AI3.A43

Indexes over 100 alternative periodicals in many fields, chiefly by subject, occasionally by author. Lists book, art, dance, theatre, film, and record reviews, articles, bibliographies, indexes, interviews, speeches, poetry, fiction. Each issue contains a list, with addresses, of titles covered. Indexes several feminist serials; articles on women by race, nationality, social and economic status, politics, employment, health, etc. form a substantial part of the publication.

137 Bulletin Signaletique.
Paris: Centre Nationale de la Recherche Scientifique, 1947- .
v.1- . Irregular.   Ref. Z7127.F7

Abstracting service which attempts world-wide coverage of
advances in various disciplines. Presently divided into subject
sections with annual indexes of authors and concepts. Brief
annotations, in French. Indexes may be searched under
"feminisme," "femme," and related terms.

138 Canadian Periodical Index.
Ottawa: Canadian Library Association, 1948- . v.1- .
Monthly.   Ref. Dept.

Author and subject index to Canadian periodicals. Useful
subject terms include: woman suffrage; women (with
subdivisions); women's liberation movement.

139 Houghton, Walter Edwards, ed.
The Wellesley Index to Victorian Periodicals, 1824-1900.
Toronto: University of Toronto Press, 1966- . 2v.
Ref. Z2005.H6

Planned as a multi-volume work that will provide indexing
for important magazines of the period. Two volumes covering
twenty major journals have been completed. Table of contents
approach with author index. Lack of a subject index (which
may be included at a later date) limits the use of the index at
this time. It is useful, however, for locating contemporary
criticism of Victorian authors.

140 Internationale Bibliographie der Zeitschriftenliteratur
(IBZ-Dietrich). 1897-1964.
Osnabruck: F. Dietrich. 1897-1964. 179v.
Ref. Dept.

Considered one of the most extensive indexes to periodical
literature in all subject areas. Published in two parts:
Abteilung A: Bibliographie der Deutschen Zeitschriftenliteratur, 1897-1964, Band 1-128. Covers important German
language periodicals, indexing over 4,000. Subjects are
arranged alphabetically, giving bibliographic information
with periodical listed by key number. Author indexes
appeared every six months. *Abteilung B:* Bibliographie der
Fremdsprachigen Zeitschriftenliteratur, 1911-1964, Band 1-51.
Alphabetical subject index to periodicals in non-German

languages 1911-1919. Annual author indexes from 1925-1964. Covers about 4,000 periodicals and reports in twenty languages from 30 different countries.

Continued by:

141 Internationale Bibliographie der Zeitschriftenliteratur aus Allen Gebieten des Wissens. International Bibliography of Periodical Literature Covering All Fields of Knowledge.
Osnabruck: F. Dietrich, 1965- . v.1- . Semiannual.
Ref. Dept.

Provides a single classified subject index to about 6,000 German and non-German periodicals. The list of periodicals indexed, subject index, and author index have been designated as Parts A, B, and C respectively. German subject headings are used.

142 Nineteenth Century Reader's Guide to Periodical Literature.
N.Y.: H. W. Wilson, 1944. 2v. Ref. Dept.

Author and subject index to fifty periodicals of a general and literary nature. Time period covered is 1890-1899, with supplementary indexing done for fourteen journals, some until as late as 1922, until they are included in other Wilson Company indexes. Invaluable for studying trends and concerns involving women during the period. Subject terms of interest are: woman; woman—history and condition; women—legal status; women—rights of women; women—social and moral questions; women as...; women in...; women's clubs.

143 Poole's Index to Periodical Literature. 1802-1906.
Boston and N.Y.: Houghton Mifflin, 1893-1908. 6v.
Ref. Dept.

Subject index to American and English nineteenth century periodicals. Items of interest are entered under the general heading "women."

144 Cumulative Author Index for Poole's Index to Periodical Literature 1802-1906.
Ann Arbor, Mich.: Pierian Press, 1971.
Ref. Dept.

145 Reader's Guide to Periodical Literature.
N.Y.: H. W. Wilson, 1900- . v.1- . Semi-monthly, monthly in July and August. Ref. Dept.

Author and subject index to U.S. periodicals of a broad, general nature. Very useful for popular level articles on a wide variety of topics relevant to women's studies. Subject terms of interest include: education of women; farm women; housewives; mothers; single women; widows; wives; women (with subdivisions); women's liberation movement.

GOVERNMENT PUBLICATIONS INDEXES

146 Canadian Government Publications. 1953-54, 1958- .
Ottawa, Ontario: Information Canada, 1953- . Monthly, cumulated annually.   **GPD RR**

Basic index to Canadian government publications, both monographs and periodicals. Divided into English and French sections, then into Parliamentary and Departmental publications sections. Useful subject headings include: abortion; discrimination; women; etc. Indexes are to both English and French sections, but there is separate indexing for monographs and periodical articles.

147 Government Publications.
London: Stationery Office, 1920- . Monthly, cumulated annually.   **GPD RR**

Basic index to publications of the British government. Entries arranged in two sections: Parliamentary (legislative) and other documents. Relevant indexing only under "women." Five year index cumulations available from 1936 to date.

148 IBID (International Bibliography, Information, Documentation).
New York: Bowker/Unipub, v.1-2, 1973-74; New York: Unipub, v.3- . 1975- . Quarterly.
          GPD RR

Volumes 1-3 indexed the sales publications of the United Nations system, i.e. the UN and all the specialized agencies, such as the International Labour Office, Unesco, the World Bank. With volume 4, the index also covers sales publications of other inter-governmental organizations. Major organizations in this category include the Organization for Economic Cooperation and Development and the Organization of the Petroleum Exporting Countries (OPEC). Entries are arranged into broad subject fields, one of which is women. Subject indexes cumulate annually.

152 Swanick, M. Lynne Struthers.
A Checklist of Canadian Federal, Provincial and Municipal
Government publications of Special Significance for Women.
Monticello, Ill., 1976. (Council of Planning Librarians
Exchange Bibliography, no. 1118)

Ref. Z5942.C68 no. 1118

Covers a wide variety of women's studies topics. Unannotated;
arranged by province.

149 Index to U.S. Government Periodicals. 1974- .
Chicago: Infordata International, 1975- . Quarterly,
cumulated annually. **GPD RR**

Subject and author index to more than 130 government
periodicals, many not indexed elsewhere. Useful subject
headings include: discrimination—sex; employment—
discrimination; employment—women; maternity; women's
movement ; and other specific topics. No annotations.

150 Monthly Catalog of United States Government Publications.
Washington, D.C.: U.S.G.P.O., 1895- . Monthly.

GPD RR

Basic index to publications of the United States government,
the most prolific publisher in the world. Entries are arranged
by the government agency which issued them. Useful subject
headings include: civil rights; discrimination; mothers;
women; women's. The library receives approximately 90%
ofthe material listed, either in paper copy or on microcards.
Monthly indexes cumulate annually. With 1974, indexes
divided by subject, title and author. Related indexes are the
Cumulative Subject Index to the Monthly Catalog, 1900-1971
and the *Checklist of United States Public Documents, 1789-
1909*, the *American Statistics Index*, and the *CIS Index*.

151 Monthly Checklist of State Publications.
Washington, D.C.: U.S. Library of Congress, 1910- . v.1- .
Monthly. **GPD RR**

Index of publications of state government agencies which have
been received by the Library of Congress. Coverage is therefore
not complete. Arrangement is by state, then by issuing agency.
Useful index terms include: discrimination; state name—
women; woman; or women ('s). Monthly issues, with no
indexes. Annual subject, author, and state indexes.

NEWS INDEXES

Newspaper Indexes

153 New York Times Index.
     · N.Y.: New York Times, Sept., 1851-Dec. 1906, 1911- .
     Semimonthly, cumulated annually.
                                 Ref. Dept.

     Reliable, contemporary guide to information on current
     events; entries include a brief synopsis of news and editorial
     matter on the topic and a precise reference to date, page, and
     column in which the item appeared. Subject headings on
     women include: labor—U.S.—women; women (with
     geographical subdivision); women's role in politics. Names of
     individual women may also be searched. There is an
     approximate lag of three months in the indexing. If the news
     item needed has been reported more recently, the New York
     Times Information Bank (at the State Library in Hartford)
     may be consulted. This data base provides computer access to
     material printed in the *New York Times* and a selected group
     of sixty-five other news periodicals from 1969 to the present.

     Other newspaper indexes are available:

154 California News Index.
     Claremont, Calif.: Center for California Public Affairs,
     1971- . v.2- . Quarterly.   Ref. Dept.

     Covers thirteen of the state's leading newspapers and
     magazines.

155 Christian Science Monitor Index.
     Boston: Christian Science Monitor, 1960- . v.1- . Monthly,
     cumulated annually.   Ref. Dept.

156 Index to Pravda.
     Columbus, Ohio: American Association for the Advancement
     of Slavic Studies, 1975- . v.1- . Monthly, cumulated
     annually.   Ref. Dept.

     Useful subjects include: Women's Committee, Soviet;
     Women's Year, International.

157 National Observer Index.
     Princeton, N.J.: Dow Jones and Co., Inc., 1970- . Annual.
                                     Ref. Dept.

158 Newspaper Index.
Wooster, Ohio: Bell and Howell Co., 1972- . Monthly.
Ref. Dept.

Indexes the *Chicago Tribune, Los Angeles Times, New Orleans Times-Picayune,* and the *Washington Post.*

159 Times, London. Official Index.
London: The Times, 1906- . Bimonthly. Frequency varies.
Ref. Dept.

Earlier years are indexed by *Palmer's Index to the Times Newspaper, 1790-1905,* available on microfilm.
Micro/Media Dept.

160 Wall St. Journal Index.
N.Y.: Dow Jones, 1958- . v.1- . Monthly, cumulated annually.
Ref. Dept.

News Services

161 Editorials on File.
N.Y.: Facts on File, Inc., 1970- . v.1- . Bimonthly.
Ref. PN4778.E3

Summaries of a given issue are followed by reprints of related editorials from selected U.S. and Canadian newspapers. Indexes are published monthly, quarterly, and annually. The heading "women's rights" is useful for searching current opinion, pro and con, on women's issues.

162 Facts on File Yearbook.
N.Y.: Facts on File, Inc., 1941- . v.1- . Weekly.
Ref. D410.F3

Digests world news developments reported in newspapers and by news services. Classified arrangement under such headings as: world affairs, national affairs, foreign affairs, finance, arts, science, education, economy, religion, etc. Indexes are published twice monthly, with annual and five year cumulations. Access by subject or name of individual.

163 Gallup Opinion Index. Report.
Princeton, N.J.: American Institute of Public Opinion, 1965- . v.1- . Monthly.   Ref. Dept.

Summarizes Gallup polls on current interest topics and social, political, and economic trends. Recent issues have featured polls on abortion, the ERA, family size, most admired woman, and women's liberation. No index.

164   Keesing's Contemporary Archives.
        London: Keesing's ltd., 1931- . v.1- . Weekly.
                              Ref. D410.K4

British news digest similar to *Facts on File* in purpose. News summaries are made from newspapers, periodicals, and official publications of the United Kingdom, the Commonwealth, foreign countries, and international news agencies. Speeches and texts of documents are often reproduced. Author and subject indexes. Subject entries are generally listed under the name of an organization or the country in which the event occurred. Useful for tracing information on international or British women's news, e.g., the International Women's Year Convention in Mexico City, listed in the subject index under "United Nations Organization."

165   What They Said; the yearbook of spoken opinion.
        Beverly Hills, Calif.: Monitor Book Co., 1970- . v.1- .
        Annual.   Ref. D410.W6

Compilation of verbal quotes of those in the public eye on various issues. Arrangement by subject, with index to speakers and subjects. "Women" and "women's rights" can be used as search terms. There is a section on women's rights included under the national affairs section of the yearbook.

Geography

166   Loyd, Bonnie.
        Women and Geography: an Annotated Bibliography and Guide to Sources of Information. Monticello, Ill., 1976. (Council of Planning Librarians Exchange Bibliography, no. 1159)   Ref. Z5942.C68 no. 1159

References to materials on women in the profession and to geographic studies on women in society.

Health and Medicine

167   Bibliography of Reproduction.

Cambridge, England: Reproduction Research Information Service. 1963- . v.1- . Monthly.

Ref. Dept.

Technical research literature on reproductive biology in vertebrates; classified arrangement, with author and animal index in each issue and subject index published twice yearly. Useful for information on the medical aspects of abortion, birth control, fertility, etc.

168 Cumulative Index to Nursing Literature.
Glendale, Calif.: Seventh Day Adventist Hospital Association. 1956- . v.1- . Bimonthly, cumulated annually.

Ref. Dept.

Subject and author index to major nursing periodicals in the English language; also selectivity indexes major medical journals. Includes a list of journals indexed and a list of subject headings used, such as: discrimination; homosexuality; married women—employment; mother-child relations; pregnancy; sex behavior; women.

169 Dollen, Charles.
Abortion in Context; a select bibliography. Metuchen, N.J.: Scarecrow, 1970.   Ref. Z7164.B5 D6

Author and title list of books and articles. Most entries date from 1967-69 and emphasize cultural, medical, and social aspects of abortion. Subject index and list of sources are included.

170 Floyd, Mary K.
Abortion Bibliography. 1970- . Troy, N.Y.: Whitson Publishing Co. Annual.   Ref. Z6671.1.A2 F57

Books and articles on abortion published during the year. Divided into title and subject sections with an author index.

171 Index Medicus.
Chicago: American Medical Assn., 1960- . v.1- . Monthly, cumulated annually to *Cumulated Index Medicus.* Continuation of *Current List of Medical Literature,* 1941-1959, v.1-36 and the *Quarterly Cumulative Index Medicus,* 1916-1956, v.1-60.   Ref. Dept.

International bibliography providing comprehensive index by subject and author to several thousand leading medical and biomedical journals. Useful subject terms include: gynecologic diseases; gynecology; obstetrics; physicians, women; pregnancy; prenatal care.

172 International Nursing Index.
N.Y.: American Journal of Nursing Co., 1966- . v.1- . Quarterly, cumulated annually. Ref. Dept.

Author and subject index to over two hundred international nursing journals as well as nursing articles from non-nursing journals indexed by *Index Medicus*. Subject terms include: abortion; gynecologic diseases; maternal health service; midwifery; obstetrical nursing; women.

173 Medical Socioeconomic Research Sources.
Chicago: American Medical Assn., 1971- . v. 1- . Quarterly, cumulated annually. Ref. Dept.

Guide to books, periodicals and other information sources on the social and economic aspects of medicine and health. Author and subject index. Topics of interest in women's studies include: abortion; birth control; child welfare; contraceptives; homosexuality; maternal welfare; physicians— wives; physicians—women; pregnancy; sex; sterilization.

174 Sharma, Prakash C.
Maternal Health and Care; a research bibliography. Monticello, Ill., 1975. (Council of Planning Librarians Exchange Bibliography, no. 725)
Ref. Z5942.C68 no. 725

Brief, unannotated list of books and periodical articles on maternal care dating from 1940-1970.

175 U.S. National Institute of Mental Health.
Women and Mental Health; a bibliography. Washington, D.C.: U.S.G.P.O., 1975. GPD HE20.8113:W84/970-973

Annotated bibliography of periodical articles, covering 1970 to 1973. Arrangement is by broad subject areas such as abortion, lesbianism, unwed mothers, etc. Author index only.

176 U.S. National Institute on Drug Abuse.
Drugs and Pregnancy; the effects of nonmedical use of drugs on pregnancy, childbirth, and neonates. Washington, D.C.: U.S.G.P.O., 1974. (Research Issues, no. 5)
GPD HE20.8214:5

Extensive annotations of approximately 100 journal articles published from 1958-1974. Included are general articles on LSD, heroin, methadone, and comparative studies of methadone and heroin. Indexing by name of drug, sample population type, geographic location, author, and subject.

177 ———.
Women and Drugs; an annotated bibliography. Washington, D.C.: U.S.G.P.O., 1975. (Special Bibliography, no. 4)
GPD HE20.8211/2:4

Annotated bibliography of 181 journal articles published between the mid-sixties and 1975. There are twelve general articles, then remainder of entries are divided into three subject groups: women and alcohol; women and narcotics; women and psychotherapeutic drug use. Author index.

178 Yale University. School of Nursing.
Nursing Studies Index; prepared under the direction of Virginia Henderson. Philadelphia: Lippincott, 1963-72. 4v. v. 1, 1900-1929; v. 2, 1930-1949; v. 3, 1950-1956; v. 4, 1957-1959.
Ref. Z6675.N7 Y3

International annotated bibliography, arranged by subject with author index, covering studies, research in progress, research methods, and historical materials in periodicals, books, and pamphlets published in the English language. Subject search terms include: abortion and nursing; fertility and sterility; gynecology and nursing; maternal health and nursing; menstruation; U.S. Women's Bureau; women.

History

179 America: History and Life.
Ed. by Eric H. Boehm. Santa Barbara, Calif.: Clio Press for the American Bibliographical Center, 1964- . v. 1- . Quarterly.
Ref. Dept.

International coverage of articles on the history and culture of the U.S. and Canada. A special supplement covers articles on the U.S. and Canada abstracted in *Historical Abstracts* from 1954-1963. Arrangement is by broad subject area with annual indexes for author, subject, biographical, and geographical entries. With 1974, the index expanded its coverage into three sections: Part A: Article Abstracts and Citations; B: Index to Book Reviews; and C: American History Index (covering books, articles, and dissertations). Subject terms include: feminism; marriage; prostitution; sex discrimination; woman suffrage; women.

180   Goodwater, Leanna.
      Women in Antiquity; an annotated bibliography. Metuchen, N.J.: Scarecrow Press, 1975.   Ref. Z7961.G66

      Extensive bibliography on the political, social, legal, and literary achievements and treatment of women in ancient Greece and Rome. Original classical sources and modern books and articles on the subject are included. Indexed by author and under the names of important ancient women.

181   Historical Abstracts; bibliography of the world's periodical literature.
      Part A: Modern History Abstracts, 1775-1914. Part B: Twentieth Century Abstracts, 1914-   . Ed. by Eric H. Boehm. Santa Barbara, Calif.: Clio Press for American Bibliographical Center, 1955-   . v. 1-   . Quarterly.
                                          Ref. Dept.

      Early volumes cover 1775-1914. In 1971, the index was divided into two parts, with coverage as noted above. U.S. and Canadian materials are excluded, beginning with 1964, as these are covered by *America: History and Life*. Abstracts are arranged by broad subject areas. Indexing by author and subject with annual and five year cumulations. "Women," with geographical subdivision, is used as a term in the subject index.

182   Leonard, Eugenie Andrus, et. al.
      The American Woman in Colonial and Revolutionary Times, 1565-1800; a syllabus with bibliography. Philadelphia: University of Pennsylvania Press, 1962.
                                    Ref. Z7964.U49 L4

      Organized to give a picture of the colonial woman in all aspects of her life and work. Religious life, education, status and rights, charitable acts, emigration, early settlement, heroic and patriotic achievements, home life, contributions to the fine arts and to industry are all covered. Arrangement by subject with references to books and articles. A list of over one hundred outstanding women of the period is included.

183 Lerner, Gerda.
     Bibliography in the History of American Women. Bronxville,
     N.Y.: Sarah Lawrence College, 1975.
                              Ref. Z7964.U49 L46 1975
     Selected reading list which grew from the author's teaching
     and research. Covers bibliographic guides, historiography,
     theories of women, a chronological history of U.S. women,
     family history, motherhood, work, education, sexuality, law,
     black women and biography as each relates to the history of
     American women. Subject arrangement; unannotated.

184 Writings on American History, 1962- .
     Washington, D.C.: American Historical Association, 1973-
     74- . Annual.   Ref. Z1236.W74
     Unannotated index to current material with chronological,
     geographical, and subject sections and an author index.
     Subject section includes women's history, classified under
     social history.

185 Writings on American History.
     Washington, D.C.: U.S.G.P.O., 1902-1961. 49v.
                              973 Am35a
     Classified bibliography of books and articles with author,
     title, and subject indexing. Gaps in publication exist for 1904-
     1905 and 1941-1947.

186 Index to the Writings on American History 1902-1940.
     Washington, D.C.: American Historical Association, 1956.
                              Ref. E174.L874

Humanities

187 American Humanities Index.
     Troy, N.Y.: Whitson Publishing Co., 1975- . v. 1- .
     Quarterly.   Ref. Dept.
     Author and subject index to scholarly and creative periodicals
     not previously covered by other indexing tools in the
     humanities. Useful headings: names of women writers,
     women poets; women's movement; women's studies.

188 British Humanities Index.
     London: Library Assn., 1962- . v. 1- . Quarterly, cumulated
     annually.   Ref. Dept.
     Subject index of about 400 British periodicals in the

humanities and social sciences, with particular emphasis on the arts and politics. Annual cumulation includes a separate author index. Education is excluded, being covered by the *British Education Index*. Many headings are relevant to women: Christianity and women; feminism; housewives; men, attitudes to women; mothers, unmarried; nuns; politician's wives; sportswomen; widows; women authors; women chefs; women cricketers, etc.; women: education; women: employment, etc.; women in poetry, etc. Successor to the *Subject Index to Periodicals*, 1915-1961.

189 Humanities Index.
N.Y.: H.W. Wilson, June, 1974- . v. 1- .
Ref. Dept.

Author and subject index to periodicals in the fields of archaeology, area studies, classics, folklore, history, language and literature, literary criticism, performing arts, philosophy, and religion. Includes a separate book review section at the back of each issue. Useful headings for women's studies include: woman; women and men; women (with subdivisions). Created by the split of the *Social Sciences and Humanities Index* and greatly increases indexing coverage of humanities periodicals.

Law

190 Congressional Information Service.
CIS Index. Washington, D.C., 1970- . Monthly, cumulated quarterly and annually.   GPD RR

Indexes and abstracts publications of Congress; hearings, reports, public laws, documents and the *Congressional Record* as it relates to specific public laws. Each subject discussed in a document and each person testifying at a hearing is indexed, in contrast with the *Monthly Catalog of U.S. Government Publications* which only indexes the main subject. Most useful headings include: women; headings beginning with women or women's; discrimination in...; and other specific subjects. The annual abstracts volume contains legislative histories. There is also a five year 1970-1974 cumulative index.

191 Index to Legal Periodicals.
New York: H.W. Wilson Company, 1926- . v. 1- . Monthly, cumulated quarterly, annually and triennially.
Ref. Dept.

Subject and author index to selected legal periodicals of the United States, Great Britain, Canada, Australia, and New Zealand, annual reviews, and yearbooks. Useful subject headings include: civil rights; discrimination; women; and other specific topics. Consult the list of subject headings and cross references in the yearly and three year cumulations. There are separate case tables and book review indexes.

192 Index to Periodical Articles Related to Law.
Dobbs Ferry, New York: Glanville Publications, 1969- . v. 11- . Quarterly, cumulated annually.
<u>Ref. Dept.</u>

Subject listing of pertinent articles in non-legal periodicals selected from journals not included in the *Index to Legal Periodicals* or the *Index to Foreign Legal Periodicals*. No annotations. Useful headings include: abortion; divorce; domestic relations; marriage; and women. Cumulation for v. 11-15, 1969-1973 available.

Literature

193 Abstracts of English Studies.
Boulder, Colorado: National Council of Teachers of English. 1958- . v. 1- . Monthly (except July and August).
<u>Ref. Dept.</u>

Annotated references are arranged in four sections: general; English; American; and world literature in English. Each section is further subdivided by period and individual author. Monthly index to names of people referred to and subjects; annual index cumulates monthly indexes with the addition of authors of articles and monographs. Useful for material on individual women authors.

194 Children's Literature Abstracts.
The Hague, Netherlands: International Federation of Library Associations, 1973- . v. 1- . Quarterly.
<u>Ref. Dept.</u>

Arranged by subject with author and subject indexes. Sexism in children's literature is one area covered.

195 Contemporary Literary Criticism.
Ed. by Carolyn Riley. Detroit: Gale Research Co., 1973- . v.1- . In progress.   <u>Ref. PN771.C584</u>

Publishes current criticism of contemporary authors by providing extracts of criticisms from books and periodical articles. Major authors, poets, and playwrights now living or deceased since 1960 are included. About two hundred authors are covered in each issue. Criticism indexed is limited to that done in the last twenty-five years. The latest volume has a cumulative index to the previous volumes by author and critic.

196   Essay and General Literature Index.
N.Y.: H.W. Wilson, 1900- . v. 1- . Semiannual, annual and quinquennial cumulations.   Ref. Dept.

Author and subject index to collections of essays. Books indexed are listed at the end of each volume. The index is useful for finding unusual or minor topics which are not likely to be covered by an entire book. For example, the 1972 volume under "women in moving pictures" has a reference to an essay on the pin-up girl. The index is also helpful for locating biographical and critical material on individuals.

197   Little Miss Muffet Fights Back; a bibliography of recommended non-sexist books about girls for young readers. Rev. ed.
N.Y.: Feminists on Children's Media, 1974.
Ref. Z1037.9.F45 1974

Annotated bibliography of books which "show girls and women as vital human beings." Divided into sections of picture books, fiction, biography, history, and women's rights.

198   Medina, José Toribio.
La Literatura Femenina en Chile. Santiago de Chile: Imprenta Universitaria, 1923.   Ref. Z1701.M49

Bibliography, in Spanish, of women authors in Chilean literature. Brief critical notes and a bibliography are given for the writers. Author index.

199   Modern Language Association of America. MLA International Bibliography.
N.Y.: Modern Language Association of America, 1921- .
Annual.
Ref. Dept.

Bibliography of significant books and articles in modern language and literature. Vol. 1: English, American, Medieval and Neo-Latin, and Celtic literatures; Vol. 2: European, Asian, African, and Latin American literatures; Vol. 3: linguistics. Within each volume, arrangement is by period, then by subject and individual author, with author index. Useful for researching material on individual authors.

200   Myers, Carol Fairbanks.
Women in Literature. Metuchen, N.J.: Scarecrow Press, 1976.
Ref. Z6514.C5 W64

Excellent, well-organized bibliography in an area of women's studies in which there is much interest. Includes writings on women characters, feminist criticism, studies of women writers, interviews with women authors, and selected reviews of works of women writers. Material included dates from 1970 to the spring of 1975. Arranged alphabetically by the name of the writer with index of critics and editors. Includes a very useful general bibliography at the end of the volume, which lists background material on women in literature.

201   Pataky, Sophie.
Lexikon Deutscher Frauen der Feder. Berlin: C. Pataky, 1898.
Ref. Biog. Z2230.5.P2

A bio-bibliography, in German, of German women authors.

202   Sense and Sensibility Collective.
Women and Literature; an annotated bibliography of women writers. 2nd. ed. Cambridge, Mass., 1973.
Ref. Z7963.L5 S4 1973

Concentrates primarily on twentieth century authors of fiction. Useful guide for personal reading and for study of recent portrayals of women in literature. Biographical notes are included for major writers Includes a useful index of topics or themes treated in the works of fiction.

Media

203   Film Literature Index.
N.Y.: Filmdex, Inc., 1973- . v. 1- . Quarterly, cumulated annually.
Ref. Dept.

Author and subject index to a selected list of film periodicals from around the world. Relevant subject headings include: actors and actresses; star system; woman in film; women filmmakers; women's rights.

204 Media Review Digest.
Ann Arbor, Mich.: Pierian Press, 1973/74-   . Annual.
Ref. Z5814.V8 M43

Index and digest of reviews of educational and popular non-book media; arranged by type (films, slides, transparencies, media kits, records, filmstrips, etc.). Contains a list of reviewing sources and a separately published subject index. (Continues *Multi Media Reviews Index* 1970-72. Ref. Z5814.V8 M85).

205 NICEM Indexes:
National Information Center for Educational Media. Los Angeles, Calif.: University of Southern California, 1973-   .
Ref. LB1043.Z9...

Series of subject indexes to media available commercially. Subject search terms include: civics and political systems—suffrage; fine arts—women in art and music; sociology—divorce. The following volumes have been published in this series:

> Index to Black History and Studies (Multimedia).
> Index to Ecology (Multimedia).
> Index to Educational Audio Tapes.
> Index to Educational Overhead Transparencies.
> Index to Educational Records.
> Index to Educational Slides.
> Index to Educational Videotapes.
> Index to 8mm Motion Cartridges.
> Index to Producers and Distributors.
> Index to Psychology (Multimedia).
> Index to 16mm Educational Films.
> Index to 35mm Educational Filmstrips.
> NICEM Update of Nonbook Media.

Philosophy

206 Philosopher's Index.
Bowling Green, Ohio: Bowling Green University, 1967- . v. 1- . Quarterly, cumulated annually.
Ref. Dept.

Indexes major U.S. and British philosophy journals, selected journals in other languages, and related interdisciplinary publications. Subject index, bibliographic data and abstracts section, and a book review index. "Women" and "sex" are used as subject headings.

Political Science, Government, and Public Affairs

207 ABC Political Science; advance bibliography of contents: political science and government.
Santa Barbara, Calif.: ABC-Clio, 1973- . v. 5- . Nine times per yer, cumulated annually. Ref. Dept.

Lists tables of contents of about 300 U.S. and foreign journals in the fields of law, political science, and related social sciences. Most issues indexed are two to six months old. Each issue is indexed by subject, with a law index and a court decisions and case notes section. Annual cumulation includes an author index. Useful subject terms: abortion; sex and sex roles; women—jobs; women—politics; women—professionals; women—status.

208 Bulletin Analytique de Documentation Politique Economique et Sociale Contemporaine.
Paris: Presses Universitaires de France, Foundation Nationale des Sciences Politiques, 1946- . v. 1- . Monthly.
Ref. Dept.

French index to about 1200 European periodicals covering political, economic, and social questions. Arrangement is classified by country, with annual subject index, but no author index. Annotated. The situation of women in various countries can be researched under "femme" with geographical subdivision.

209 International Bibliography of Political Science.
London: Tavistock; Chicago: Aldine, 1953- . v. 1- . Annual.
Ref. Dept.

Part of the UNESCO *International Bibliography of the Social Sciences*, this is a selective, classified listing of books, periodical articles, pamphlets, and documents with author and subject indexes. Although there is about a two year lag in indexing of materials, still an essential, high quality tool for political science research. "Women in politics" is used as a subject heading.

210　International Political Science Abstracts.
　　　Oxford: Blackwell, 1951- . v. 1- . Bimonthly.
　　　　　　　　　　　　　　　　　Ref. Dept.

Covers over four hundred of the world's significant journals in political science and related disciplines. Classified arrangement with author and subject indexes which are cumulated annually. "Women" and "women's liberation movement" are terms used in the subject index.

211　Levenson, Rosaline.
　　　Women in Government and Politics; a bibliography of American and foreign sources. Monticello, Ill., 1973. (Council of Planning Librarians Exchange Bibliography, no. 491)
　　　　　　　　　　　　　　Ref. Z5942.C68 no. 491

Main emphasis on women's contributions to politics and government in the United States after 1940. Arrangement by subject, with detailed breakdown, e.g., women in the armed forces, police, foreign service, congress, women as judges, diplomats, etc. No index.

212　Levitt, Morris.
　　　Women's Role in American Politics. Monticello, Ill., 1973. (Council of Planning Librarians Exchange Bibliography, no. 446)　　　　　　　　　　Ref. Z5942.C68 no. 446

Brief, general listing of publications on the effects of work, education, and marriage on the political role of women in the United States in the last two decades.

213　Peace Research Abstracts Journal.
　　　Clarkson, Ontario: Canadian Peace Research Institute, 1964- . v. 1- . Monthly.　　　Ref. Dept.

Despite the use of an intricately classified and coded arrangement, this is a valuable tool for international relations literature. Major classifications are: the military situation; limitation of arms; tension and conflict; ideology and issues; international institutions and regional alliances; nations and national policies; diplomacy; decision making and communications; methods of study; bibliographies and other general literature. Monthly and annual author indexes and an annual subject index ordered by classification code number, for example, Section IX-46: "Decision Making and Communications—Role of Women in National Decisions."

214 Public Affairs Information Service (PAIS), Bulletin.
N.Y.: Public Affairs Information Service, Inc., 1915- . v. 1- .
Weekly, cumulated quarterly and annually.
Ref. Dept.

Subject index of books, pamphlets, government publications, and periodical articles published in English which concern economic and social conditions, international relations, etc. Emphasis is on factual and statistical information. Subject headings relevant to women are quite extensive and include: delinquent girls; directories—women; employment—wives; employment—women; executive's wives; housewives; mothers; Negro women; policewomen; U.S.—armed forces— women; wages and salaries—women; wives; women (with subdivisions); women's liberation movement.

215 Swanick, M. Lynne Struthers.
Women in Canadian Politics and Government; a bibliography. Monticello, Ill., 1974. (Council of Planning Librarians Exchange Bibliography, no. 697)
Ref. Z5942.C68 no. 697

Listings of articles, books, and documents on the roles and rights of women in Canadian politics and government. Arranged by author with brief subject index. A list of government bodies concerned with Canadian women and a list of current periodicals by and concerning Canadian women are also provided.

216 U.S. Council of National Defense. Woman's Committee.
Woman in the War; a bibliography. Washington, D.C.: U.S.G.P.O., 1918.   GPD Y3.C83:62/W19/4

Contemporary books, periodical articles, government publications, and newspaper articles on women's service in World War I. There is a short list of bibliographies. Basic arrangement corresponds to the structure of the Woman's Committee; so sections deal with education, food administration, food production, health and recreation, and women in industry. Further breakdowns are by country. There is a short section on women in other wars. No indexes.

Population

217 Current Literature in Family Planning.

N.Y.: Planned Parenthood, 1974- . v. 64- . Monthly.

<u>Ref. Dept.</u>

Annotated subject list of books and articles on U.S. family planning which are received in the Katharine Dexter McCormick Library, Planned Parenthood-World Population Information and Education Department. Good current awareness tool for population issues, but its usefulness for retrospective searching is limited due to lack of indexing.

218 Driver, Edwin D.
World Population Policy; and annotated bibliography. Lexington, Mass.: Lexington Books, 1971.

<u>Ref. Z7164.D3 D75</u>

Listing of publications concerned with general population policy and measures affecting fertility and family size. Scope is international, and covers publications of 1940-1969. Arrangement is geographic, with author and subject indexing. Subject search terms: abortion; birth control; contraception; divorce; family planning; marriage; mothers; pregnancy; women.

219 Family Planning/Population Reporter.
Washington: Center for Family Planning Program Development, Planned Parenthood-World Population, Oct., 1973- . v. 2, no. 5- . Bimonthly.

<u>Ref. KF3771.A73 F3</u>

Review of state laws and policies with news highlights of developments in state and U.S. legislation and court cases. A current awareness tool for material on abortion, family planning, maternity leave policies, sterilization, etc. Unfortunately, there is no index.

220 Population Index.
Princeton, N.J.: Office of Population Research, Princeton University and Population Association of America, 1935- . v. 1- . Quarterly.   <u>Ref. Dept.</u>

Annotated listing of world-wide books and periodical articles on all phases of population. Classified arrangement, with annual cumulated indexes by author and country. No subject index. Some sections relevant to women include: fertility and natural increase (including fertility controls); marriage, divorce, and the family.

221 Sharma, Prakash C.
Family Planning Programs; a selected international research bibliography. Monticello, Ill., 1974. (Council of Planning Librarians Exchange Bibliography. no. 556)
                                    Ref. Z5942.C68 no. 556

Very brief, unannotated list of 250 references on family planning programs from 1968-1973. Included are books and monographs, articles, research reports, and conference proceedings.

Psychology

222 Child Development Abstracts and Bibliography.
Chicago: University of Chicago Press for the Society for Research in Child Development, 1927- . v. 1- . Three times a year.   Ref. Dept.

Covers about 140 U.S. and foreign periodicals in biology, psychology, education, medicine, and public health for relevant child development articles. Some books are abstracted also. Classified arrangement with author and subject indexes. Many relevant listings on such topics as working mothers, sex roles, etc.

223 Psychological Abstracts.
Washington, D.C.: American Psychological Association, Inc., 1927- . v. 1- . Monthly.   Ref. Dept.

Classified bibliography to the world's literature in psychology and related disciplines. Author and subject indexes are cumulated twice a year. Subject terms include: female criminals; femininity; housewives; sex roles; wives; women; women's liberation movement. Cumulated index as follows:

Author Index to "Psychological Index," 1894-1935, and "Psychological Abstracts," 1927-1958. 5v.
———— 1st suppl., 1959-1963. 1v.
———— 2nd suppl., 1964-1968. 2v.
———— 3rd suppl., 1969-1971. 1v.
———— 4th suppl., 1972-1974. 1v.

Cumulated Subject Index to "Psychological Abstracts," 1927-1960. 2v.
———— 1st suppl., 1961-1965. 1v.
———— 2nd suppl., 1966-1968. 2v.

_____ 3rd suppl., 1969-1971. 2v.
_____ 4th suppl., 1972-1974. 2v.

Religion

224 American Theological Library Association.
     Index to Religious Periodical Literature. Chicago: American
     Theological Library Association, 1949- . v. 1- . Semi-
     annual.   Ref. Z7753.A5

     Author and subject index, with Protestant emphasis, to major
     religious and some archaeological journals in the U.S. and
     Europe. Contains a separate book review index. Many
     women's issues are covered, including: abortion; divorce;
     lesbianism; marriage; mothers; religious orders, women's; sex;
     sex and religion; sex role; single women; woman; women as
     ministers; women in Christianity; women in the Bible.

225 Catholic Periodical and Literature Index.
     Haverford, Pa.: Catholic Library Association, 1930- . v. 1- .
     Bimonthly, cumulated biennially.
                                          Ref. Z7837.C32

     Author and subject index to Catholic periodicals and selection
     of Catholic-interest books with descriptive annotations.
     Women's issues covered include: abortion; divorce;
     homosexuality, marriage; mothers; ordination of women; sex;
     woman (with subdivisions); women as ministers; women in
     the Bible; women's liberation movement. Continues the
     Catholic Periodical Index and absorbs the _Guide to Catholic
     Literature._

226 Index to Jewish Periodicals.
     Columbia Heights, Ohio: College of Jewish Studies Press,
     June, 1963- . v. 1- . Annual. Ref. Z6367.I5

     Author and subject index to about fifty Jewish journals, both
     general and scholarly. Subjects of interest include: abortion;
     women, Jewish; women and Judaism; women as rabbis;
     women in politics; women in the Bible; women in the
     Talmud; women (Jewish law); women's liberation movement.

227 Religious and Theological Abstracts.
     Myerstown, Pa.: Religious and Theological Abstracts, Inc.,
     1958- . v. 1- . Quarterly.   Ref. Z7751.R4

Nonsectarian index to about 150 religious periodicals in various languages. Biblical, theological, historical, and practical sections, with a new sociological section added in the spring of 1975. Annual subject, author, and scripture indexes. Subject terms: abortion; divorce; homosexuality; marriage; sex; sexuality; women, ministry of; women, role of; women's liberation movement.

Science and Technology

228　Applied Science and Technology Index.
　　　N.Y.: H. W. Wilson, 1958- . v. 1- . Monthly (except July), cumulated annually.　　　Ref.Dept.

　　　Subject index to selected English language periodicals. Although major emphasis is on the scientific and technical areas, articles can be found dealing with the employment of women as engineers, physicists, scientists, etc., women in various industries, the changing pattern of employment for women, and educational programs which encourage/discourage women. Formerly entitled *Industrial Arts Index*, 1913-1957.

229　Biological Abstracts; reporting the world's biosciences research. Philadelphia: Biological Abstracts, 1927- . v. 1- . Semimonthly.　　　Ref. Dept.

　　　Covering over 8,000 periodicals and other materials. Classified arrangement with subject, author, generic, systematic, and cross indexes. Subject index is computer-generated from title and key words. Useful for researching medical and biological topics of concern to women.

230　Biological and Agricultural Index.
　　　N.Y.: H. W. Wilson, 1964- . v. 19- . Continues *Agricultural Index*, 1916-64. v. 1-18. Monthly (except August), cumulated annually.　　　Ref. Dept.

　　　Subject index to selected English language periodicals in the field. Indexing terms include: clothing and dress; education of women; farm women; mothers; women—employment; women—physiology; women as dairy farmers; women's clubs.

231　Current Contents.
　　　Philadelphia: Institute for Scientific Information, 1974- . v. 6- . Weekly.　　　Ref. Dept.

This series provides up-to-date indexing of scientific literature by reproducing tables of contents of domestic and foreign journals in various fields. Of interest in women's studies are *Current Contents: Life Sciences* and *Current Contents: Social and Behavioral Sciences*. There is an author index (with addresses) and subject index by key title words. Indexes of journals included are published periodically.

232   Roysdon, Christy.
      Women in Engineering; a bibliography on their progress and prospects. Monticello, Ill., 1975. (Council of Planning Librarians Exchange Bibliography, no. 878).
                                        Ref. Z5942.C68 no. 878

Books, journal articles, conference reports, and government and association publications are included. Entries organized by subjects such as the status of women engineers, recruitment, education, and training. Some background information on the professional woman in general is also included.

Social Sciences

233   Social Sciences and Humanities Index.
      N.Y.: H. W. Wilson, 1907-1974. v. 1-27. Quarterly.
                                        Ref. Dept.

Author and subject index to about two hundred scholarly journals in the fields of anthropology, archaeology, classics, economics, history, geography, language, literature, philosophy, political science, and religion. Subject headings of interest include: Amazons; convents and nunneries; divorce; single women; unmarried mothers; women (with subdivisions); women's liberation movement. Formerly titled *International Index to Periodicals*, 1907-1964. Continued by the *Humanities Index* and the *Social Sciences Index*.

234   Social Sciences Citation Index.
      Philadelphia: Institute for Scientific Information, 1969- .
      Three times a year, cumulated annually.
                                        Ref. Dept.

International index to ranking journals in the social sciences. The rationale behind this index is that the publications which an author cites are earlier works of significance on the same topic. Arranged in three sections: source index which gives full bibliographic description under the author's name;

citation index which lists all items cited in the author's bibliography by authors of these items; and permuterm subject index which pairs significant terms in the titles of articles indexed. For example, an entry under feminism paired with psychoanalysis leads to an article listed in the source index under the author's name, M. Ash, called "Psychoanalysis and Feminism." A researcher with a known reference on a topic can also search the citation index for others using the same item in their work.

235 Social Sciences Index.
       N.Y.: H. W. Wilson, June, 1974- . v. 1- . Quarterly.
                                              Ref. Dept.

One of the two new indexes which supersede the *Social Sciences and Humanities Index*. It increases to 263 the number of periodicals indexed in the social science field. Indexing by author and subject. Useful headings in addition to "women" are: abortion; dating (social custom); day care centers; delinquent women; prostitution; women's liberation movement.

Sociology

CRIMINOLOGY

236 Abstracts on Criminology and Penology.
       Deventer, the Netherlands: published by Kluwer for Criminological Foundation. 1969- . v. 9- . Bimonthly.
                                              Ref. Dept.

International abstracting journal containing a feature article in each issue followed by a classified bibliography of books and periodical articles. Author and subject indexes cumulate annually. Excellent source of information on women and crime, women in prison. Consult subject index under "female." Formerly entitled *Excerpta Criminologica*, 1961-68, v. 1-8.

237 Crime and Delinquency Abstracts.
       Chevy Chase, Md.: National Institute of Mental Health, 1965-1972, v. 2-8.   Ref. Dept.

Covered scientific and professional literature including research reports. Author and subject index cumulated annually. The keyword subject index can be searched under such terms as: female; girls; rape; women, etc. Formerly titled *International Bibliography on Crime and Delinquency*.

238   Crime and Delinquency Literature.
      Paramus, N.J.: National Council on Crime and Delinquency,
      1968- . v. 1- . Quarterly.   Ref. Dept.

      Each issue contains a valuable comprehensive review of
      significant world-wide literature on a particular topic in
      criminology. The female offender, e.g., was covered in
      December, 1970 and in March, 1975. Sex offenders and
      victimless crime (including prostitution) are other areas
      covered. Subject index.

239   Davis, Lenwood G.
      The Policewoman in American Society. Monticello, Ill., 1976.
      (Council of Planning Librarians Exchange Bibliography, no.
      1045)   Ref. Z5942.C68 no. 1045

      Brief, unannotated list of books, articles, pamphlets,
      government documents, theses, and dissertations.

THE FAMILY

240   Aldous, Joan and Reuben Hill.
      International Bibliography of Research in Marriage and the
      Family. Minneapolis: University of Minnesota for the
      Minnesota Family Life Study Center and the Institute of Life
      Insurance. v. 1, 1900-1964, 1967. v. 2, compiled by Joan Aldous
      and Nancy Dahl, 1965-1972, 1974.
                                 Ref. Z7164.M2 A48

      Computer-produced author and key word subject
      bibliography which attempts to index all significant family
      research published in books, articles, and pamphlets. Very
      valuable for research on women in the family. Arranged in
      several sections: volume one has a keyword in context index; a
      classified subject index; a complete reference list; an author
      index; and a periodicals list. Volume two has a keyword in
      context index; subject index; author list containing the
      complete bibliographical citation; and a periodicals list.

241   Inventory of Marriage and Family Literature.
      St. Paul, Minn.: Family Social Science, University of
      Minnesota, 1975. v. 3- . 1973/74- . Annual.
                                 Ref. Z7164.M2 I5

      Continuation of the *International Bibliography of Research
      in Marriage and the Family.* Classified subject arrangement
      with subject, author, and key word indexes.

242 American Home Economics Association.
   Family Relations and Child Development. Washington,
   1966- . Annual.   Ref. Z5775.A4235

   Compilation of abstracts of masters and doctoral theses in
   home economics; part of the Home Economics Research
   Abstracts series. A classified arrangement in two sections, one
   for family relations and one for child development. Author
   index. Relevant topics include: childcare services; husband-
   wife relationships; marriage role expectations.

243 Goode, William J. et. al.
   Social Systems and Family Patterns. Indianapolis: Bobbs-
   Merrill Co., Inc., 1971.   Ref. HM17.G66

   Compilation of research findings from the standard literature
   of anthropology, sociology, and psychology. Arranged in the
   form of a "propositional inventory" which attempts to
   correlate factors affecting the family and give references supporting the correlation. For example, under:
      Abortion
        x Rank of women
   is given the proposition, "The abortion rate will rise with the
   increasing independence of women." A reference to an item
   supporting this statement is then given. Many areas of interest
   in women's studies are treated, e.g., age at marriage, child
   rearing attitudes, independence of women, role behavior of
   wife, etc.

244 Hu, Teh-wei.
   Selected Bibliography on Child Care Evaluation Studies.
   Monticello, Ill., 1973. (Council of Planning Librarians
   Exchange Bibliography, no. 440)
                        Ref. Z5942.C68 no. 440
   Very brief, unannotated list of references on day care.

245 McKenney, Mary.
   Divorce; a selected annotated bibliography. Metuchen, N.J.:
   Scarecrow Press, 1975.   Ref. Z7164.M2 M34

   Bibliography of writings on divorce in books, pamphlets, and
   periodical articles. Divided into broad subject areas (legal,
   financial, psychological aspects, etc.) with annotations
   reflecting the author's stated feminist point of view. Subject
   and author index, appendices of organizations concerned with
   divorce, and divorce laws by state are included.

246   Schlesinger, Benjamin.
      The One Parent Family; perspectives and annotated
      bibliography. 3rd. ed. Toronto: University of Toronto Press,
      1975.   Ref. HQ535.S27 1975

      Essays on the one parent family and an annotated
      bibliography of materials published on the topic in two
      sections, one covering 1930-1969 and the other 1970-1974.
      Author index.

247   Strugnell, Cécile.
      Adjustment to Widowhood and some Related Problems. N.Y.:
      Health Sciences Publishing Corp., 1974.
                                   Ref. Z7961.S54 1974

      Annotated bibliography on widowhood developed from the
      work of the Widow to Widow Program at Harvard University.
      Arranged alphabetically by author in subject sections such as
      bereavement, loneliness, the role of women, and mutual help
      groups.

GENERAL

248   Current Sociology.
      The Hague: Mouton, 1952- . v. 1- . Three times a year
      (varies).   Ref. Dept.

      Reviews the literature of individual topics and research in the
      field of sociology. Issues treat a different sociological topic,
      e.g., v. 17, 1969 deals with the sociology of marriage and
      family behavior, with bibliographic citations to items on the
      family and sex roles, women's status, and men's and women's
      marital roles. These reviews, based on the accumulated
      literature, produce a succession of definitive bibliographies on
      such topics as the sociology of the family, sociology of mental
      illness, military sociology, political sociology, etc. Reports on
      the topic are followed by a bibliography. Author index.

249   Human Resources Abstracts.
      Beverly Hills, Calif.: Sage, 1966- . v. 1- . Quarterly.
                                   Ref. Dept.

      Covers articles, books, government and unpublished reports.
      Feature articles on current problems are also included.
      Arrangement is classified, with cumulative author and subject
      indexes. Useful for issues related to city and national
      problems, welfare, etc. Formerly *Poverty and Human
      Resources Abstracts*, 1966-1974, v. 1-9.

250 International Bibliography of Sociology.
   London: Tavistock; Chicago: Aldine, 1951- . v. 1- . Annual.
                                          Ref. Dept.

   List of significant international books, pamphlets, articles,
   and government publications. Volumes 1 to 4 are included in
   Current Sociology. In 1955, this bibliography split off as a
   separate publication and became part of the *International
   Bibliography of the Social Sciences*. Classified arrangement,
   with author and subject indexes. Time lag in publication is
   about two years. Subject index terms include: equal
   opportunity; feminism; married women; matriarchy;
   sexuality; woman worker; women's rights; women's status.

251 Sociological Abstracts.
   N.Y.: Sociological Abstracts, 1953- . v. 1- . Five times per
   year.   Ref. Dept.

   Classified, international abstracting journal for sociology and
   related disciplines. Two of the classified sections are pertinent:
   "Feminist studies" and "The family and socialization."
   Conference papers presented at meetings of national and
   international societies are often abstracted and published as
   supplements. Author and subject indexes are cumulated
   annually.

SEXUALITY

252 Business and Professional Women's Foundation.
   Sex Role Concepts: How Women and Men See Themselves
   and Each Other; a selected annotated bibliography, by Jeanne
   Spiegel. Washington, 1969.   Ref. Z7164.S42 B84

   Brief but useful bibliography lists material published between
   1959 and 1969. Includes popular articles as well a scholarly
   studies. Arranged alphabetically by author.

253 Damon, Gene, and Lee Stuart.
   The Lesbian in Literature; a bibliography. San Francisco,
   Calif.: Daughters of Bilitis, Inc., 1967.
                                          Spec. WZ90

   Alphabetical listing by author of all known books of general
   literature in the English language concerned with lesbianism.
   Includes novels, short stories, poems, drama, fictionalized
   biography, and some items of biography, autobiography and
   general works. A letter and asterisk coding system tells the

searcher both the amount and the quality of the lesbian material in the work. Each item was examined by the compilers; several are annotated.

254 Damon, Gene, Jan Watson, and Robin Jordan.
The Lesbian in Literature; a bibliography. 2nd ed. Reno, Nevada: The Ladder, 1975.   Spec. WZ141

Differs from the first edition in the elimination of over 3,000 items in the "trash" category, and increased inclusion of biographical, autobiographical, and other non-fiction items selected for their accuracy.

255 Parker, William.
Homosexuality; a selective bibliography of over 3,000 items. Metuchen, N.J.: Scarecrow Press, 1971.
Ref. Z7164.S42 P35

Extensive listing, arranged by type of publication. Indexed by author and subject. Lesbianism, masculinity-feminity, gender identity and role are some of the areas treated.

256 Reyna, Magdalena B.
Lesbianism and Male Homosexuality; a bibliography. Storrs: University of Connecticut, 1973.
Ref. Z7164.S42 R44

Brief, unannotated listing of books and articles on lesbianism, with a few general items on male homosexuality.

257 Seruya, Flora C., et. al.
Sex and Sex Education; a bibliography. N.Y.: R. R. Bowker, 1972.   Ref. Z7164.S42 S38

Subject listing, composed mainly of books, on such topics as sex attitudes, customs and behavior, psychology of sex, etc. Author, title, and subject indexes.

258 U.S. National Institute of Mental Health.
Sex Roles; a research bibliography by Helen S. Astin, Allison Parelman and Anne Fisher. Washington, D.C.: U.S.G.P.O., 1975.   GPD HE20.8113:Se9

Lengthy abstracts of 350 journal articles and 100 books or chapters published from 1960-1972. Covers development of sex differences and sex roles, sex roles in institutions, and cross-cultural overviews of the status of the sexes. Author and subject indexes.

259 Weinberg, Martin S. and Alan P. Bell, eds.
Homosexuality; an annotated bibliography. N.Y.: Harper and Row, 1972.   Ref. Z7164.S42 W425

List of over 1200 books and articles in English, published between 1940-1968, which concentrate on the physiological, psychological, and sociological aspects of homosexuality. Popular material is excluded. Author and subject indexes.

URBAN AFFAIRS

260 Davis, Lenwood G.
Black Women in the Cities, 1872-1972. Monticello, Ill., 1972. (Council of Planning Librarians Exchange Bibliography, no. 336)   Ref. Z5942.C68 no. 336

Selective bibliography dealing with the life and achievements of black women in U.S. cities. Included are books, articles, reports, and pamphlets, government documents, general reference works, selected black periodicals, U.S. libraries with black history collections, U.S. journals concerned with urban affairs, and related Council of Planning Librarians' bibliographies.

———.

Black Women in the Cities, 1872-1975. 2nd ed. Monticello, Ill., 1975. (Council of Planning Librarians Exchange Bibliography, no. 751-752)   Ref. Z5942.C68 no. 751-752

Updates and expands the first edition and also includes a list of black women's national organizations and a listing of black women elected officials.

261 Index to Current Urban Documents.
Westport, Ct.: Greenwood Press, 1972- . v. 1- . Quarterly.
Ref. Z7165.U5 I654

Covers both municipal and county documents issued by selected large cities and counties in the U.S. and Canada. Arranged by place and issuing agency; second section by subject. Geographic and subject indexes and a list of cities and counties indexes are included. Subject index includes listings under "employment—women" and "women."

262 Sage Urban Studies Abstracts.
Beverly Hills and London: Sage Publications, 1973- . v. 1- .
Quarterly.   Ref. Dept.

Books, articles, government documents, pamphlets, speeches and other "fugitive" materials are included. Classified arrangement with author and subject indexes.

FEMINIST SERIALS IN THE UNIVERSITY OF CONNECTICUT LIBRARY'S ALTERNATIVE PRESS COLLECTION

by Joanne V. Akeroyd

The 102 titles listed in the following section represent the feminist periodicals in the Alternative Press Collection at the University of Connecticut Library. Although the collection is not exhaustive, it is substantial, and represents well the different philosophies and publishing outlets of the women's movement. Included after the title and imprint in this list are the collection's holdings as of January, 1977. In cases where very few issues are held, the annotations list the topics of the major articles in these issue, in that way allowing this bibliography to serve as a partial index to these articles. The collection is continually growing, and inquiries are welcome.

263   Ain't I a Woman?

Iowa City, Ia.: AIAW Collective. v. 2:8, 2:9 (1972). Twelve issues a year.

Tabloid with articles on Joan Bird of the New York 21, communities, age chauvinism and children's liberation, structuring a revolution, poetry, announcements of feminist events and publications.

264   Albatross: The Radical-Lesbian-Feminist-Satire-Sarcasm-Magazene.

East Orange, N.J.: Albatross Collective. Oct. (1975).

Short articles, cartoons, ads, announcements, letters, quizzes, and book and restaurant reviews, mostly satirical.

265   Alert: Women's Legislative Review.

Middletown, Conn. v. 1:4 (1973)- 4:1 (1976). Monthly.

Tabloid reporting on women in politics, legislation and court cases involving women, some general articles, calendar of events. Ceased publication.

266 Amazon Quarterly.
     Somerville, Mass.: Amazon Press. v. 1:1 (1972)-3:2 (1975).
     Quarterly.

     Literary and arts quarterly with a lesbian/feminist
     perspective. Includes book reviews and bibliographies. Vol. 3,
     no. 1 has an annotated directory of feminist presses. Ceased
     publication.

267 American Library Association. Social Responsibilities Round
     Table. Task Force on the Status of Women in Librarianship.
     Newsletter.
     New York, N.Y. v. 1:3 (1971), 1:4, 2:1 (1972).

     Reports on activities, meetings, and resources of concern to
     women librarians and pertaining to feminist programs and
     materials in libraries. Continued as *Women in Libraries*.

268 Aphra: Feminist Literary Magazine.
     New York, N.Y. v. 1:1 (1969)- . Quarterly.

     Includes poetry, short fiction, photography, essays. Described
     in *Amazon Quarterly* as tending toward "academia and
     heterosexual values."

269 Atalanta.
     Storrs, Conn.: University of Connecticut Women's Center. v.
     1:1 (1975)-(Dec. 1975). Irregular.

     Tabloid with articles concerning the UConn community and
     national trends and events of concern to the women's
     movement; classifieds, reviews. Was published jointly with
     Alert; ceased publication.

270 Aurora: Prism of Feminism.
     Suffern, N.Y.: Rockland County Feminists. Winter (1971).
     Quarterly.

     Articles of social and political commentary, sexism, ageism,
     children's literature, day care, reviews, poetry, ads and
     announcements.

271 Battle Acts.
     New York, N.Y.: Women of Youth Against War and Fascism.
     v. 1:1 (1970)-2:4 (1972). Bimonthly.

     An angry magazine with articles on welfare, unwed mothers,
     factory and sales workers' conditions, Rockefeller, drugs,
     women of Ireland, prison, day care, AT&T conditions, food,
     cost of living, and reports of movement activity.

272   Big Mama Rag.
      Denver, Co.: BMR Collective. v. 1:2 (1973)- . Monthly.

      Newspaper with news, feature articles, columns, media
      reviews, announcements and ads of Colorado local and
      national feminist interest.

273   Black Women's Log.
      Springfield, Mass.: Sisterhood Alliance Media, Inc. Aug. 1974.
      Monthly.

      Contains articles, poetry, media reviews, letters, crossword
      puzzles, bibliographies, and shared experiences to resist
      racism, sexism, and self-oppression. Appears to have ceased
      publication.

274   Broadsheet: New Zealand's Feminist Magazine.
      Auckland, New Zealand. Broadsheet Group of Auckland's
      Women's Liberation. no. 30 (June 1975). Monthly.

      Contains articles on rape, International Women's Year,
      payment for housework, Tupperware parties, abortion and
      health care in New Zealand, Vietnamese women,
      consciousness raising, poetry, fiction, ads.

275   Change: A Working Women's Newspaper.
      San Francisco, Calif. v. 1:4, 1:5 (1971), 2:3 (1972). Irregular.

      Tabloid issued by women angry about women's working
      conditions, and anti-ERA. Articles discuss sex discrimination
      in different companies, women's attempts to organize, welfare,
      auto-repair.

276   Coyote (Calls, Howls, Growls, etc.): the Newsletter of a Loose
      Women's Organization.
      San Francisco, Calif.: Coyote: Margo St. James. v. 1:1
      (1974)- .

      Newsletter of Coyote (Call Off Your Tired Old Ethics),
      containing articles, comics, awards, letters, and announce-
      ments, chiefly concerned with the ironies and hypocrisies
      resulting from laws against prostitution.

277   Do It NOW.
      Chicago, Ill.: National Organization for Women. v. 8:1-3
      (1975). Bimonthly.

      Newsmagazine from the NOW National Office. Reports on

NOW's local and national activities and legislative news of concern to women. Contains feminist ads and job listings.

278 The Eagle.
Alderson, W. Va.: Federal Reformatory for Women. v. 1:6 (1973)-2:5 (1974). Monthly.

Mimeographed prison magazine/newsletter containing poetry, short fiction, and prisoner-related articles (health, parole boards, halfway houses, prison life) and announcements.

279 Electronics Blues.
Santa Clara, Calif. no. 1 (1971?); no. 2 (1971).

Tabloid issued by women working in electronics companies asserting their grievances, including a quiz on "creeping companyism."

280 Erato.
Storrs, Conn. v. 2:2 (April 1975), edited by Bessy Reyna and Ellen Stone.

Magazine of poetry written by women primarily from the University community. Sponsored by the University of Connecticut Women's Center, Women's Studies, and Continuing Education for Women.

281 Everywoman.
Los Angeles, Calif. v. 1:1 (1970)-1:32 (1972). Monthly.

Tabloid format, but with many long, analytical articles (on GI's and Asian women, women in other countries, J.S. Mill, prisons, health, sex, abortion, women in history), fiction, poetry, media reviews, letters, ads, and announcements. Ceased publication.

282 Feelings: From Women's Liberation.
Brooklyn, N.Y.: Feelings. no. 1 (1970).

Magazine of poetry, fiction, discussion (consciousness raising, man-hating, secretarial work), and random observations.

283 Feminist Art Journal.
Brooklyn, N.Y. v. 1:1 (1972)- . Some issues missing. Quarterly.

Contends that sexist prejudice and ignorance have written out or off women's art. Articles present, interpret, and promote the visual, literary, and aural products of women artists, past and present, in articles, interviews, and illustrations. Includes letters, classifieds, reviews, ads, and announcements.

284 The Feminist Voice.
Chicago, Ill.: Feminist Voice Collective. v. 1:9, 1:10 (1972). Monthly.

Tabloid of articles on shared experiences, women in colleges, sexism in schools, abortion, women in history, cartoons, the ERA, classified ads, directories, events calendars.

285 Fighting Woman News.
New York: Valerie Eads. March (1976).

Newsletter on women in the martial arts, self-defense, and combative sports, with articles, media reviews, letters, pertinent ads.

286 The Flowered Fist.
Storrs, Ct.: UConn Gay Alliance. no. 1 (1973).

Two-page newsletter introduces the Alliance and its point of view to the UConn community.

287 Focus: A Journal For Gay Women.
Boston, Mass.: Boston Daughters of Bilitis. v. 2:4 (1971)- . Monthly.

Magazine/newsletter with reports on DOB activities, letters, articles, poetry, stories, reviews, ads, and announcements for women's and gay publications and events. Continues *Maiden Voyage*.

288 Full Moon.
Northampton, Mass. no. 1 ([Sept.?] 1972).

Tabloid with articles on welfare, Appalachian women, population control, women at Westover AFB, waitressing, WACs, crossword puzzle, poetry, source directory.

289 The Furies: Lesbian/Feminist Monthly.
Washington, D.C. no. 1-3, 5 (1972). Bimonthly.

Tabloid of long articles on the politics, psychology, and shared experiences of lesbianism, poetry, women in history, ads, media reviews.

290   Hera: A Philadelphia Feminist Publication.
      Philadelphia, Pa.: Hera, Inc. Indian Summer 1975, 1977-   .

      Feminist newspaper with substantial analytical articles of
      national and local concern (International Women's Year
      Conference, third world women, Feminist Media Union,
      Sagaris, housework, Steinem/Redstockings, Socialist Feminist
      Conference), poetry, art, and announcements of events,
      publications, media programs.

291   Human Rights For Women. HRW Newsletter.
      Washington, D.C. no. 6 (1971).

      Brief items listing current status of bills, court cases, projects,
      meetings, and publications concerning women's rights.

292   Hysteria.
      Cambridge, Mass.: Media Center. v. 1:3 (1970)-1:6 (1971).

      Newspaper containing articles on most aspects of the women's
      movement, announcements and poetry.

293   KNOW News.
      Pittsburgh, Pa.: KNOW, Inc. v. 6:1 (1975). Irregular.

      Newsletter from a feminist publishing concern, with feature
      articles on women's rights (e.g., Black women in higher
      education), publications lists, conference announcements.
      Collection also contains their publication catalogs.

294   Kaleidoscope.
      Niantic, Ct.: Connecticut Correctional Institution for Women.
      Fall (1970); Winter (1972).

      An inmate publication containing articles, interviews,
      anecdotes, poetry, art work, stories, health care tips.

295   Labor Pains Newsletter: about the Politics of Child Care.
      Cambridge, Mass. no. 8 (April 23, 1975).

      Newsletter with articles on working mothers, welfare mothers,
      child care, and day care.

296   The Ladder.
      San Francisco, Calif.; Reno, Nev.: Daughters of Bilitis. v. 1:6
      (1957)-16:11/12 (1972). Some issues missing. Bimonthly.

      Lesbian magazine published for 16 years; began in 1956 as the
      only one in the U.S., and ceased with v. 16, no. 11/12, 1972.

Contains articles, poetry, interviews, fiction, reviews, and bibliographies.

297 Lavender Vision.
Cambridge, Mass.: Media Center. v. 1:2 (1971). Irregular.

Tabloid of lesbian poetry, letters, articles on Vietnamese women, coming out, macho, monogamy, ads and announcements.

298 Lesbian Connection.
East Lansing, Mich.: Ambitious Amazons. v. 1:4 (1975)- . Irregular.

Newsletter to announce and report on events and concerns in lesbian communities, and to act as a forum for dialog among lesbians. Articles include the American Lesbian Medical Association, lesbians and alcoholism, lesbian mothers, Montreal Lesbian Conference, reviews, and announcements.

299 Lesbian Herstory Archives Newsletter.
New York, N.Y. no. 2 (1976)- .

Newsletter of an important research oriented project, with information on lesbian materials in the archive, research queries, and bibliographies.

300 Lesbian Tide.
Santa Monica, Calif.: Tide Collective. v. 3:7 (1974)- . Some issues missing. Bimonthly.

Radical feminist lesbian magazine with national and local news, feature articles, poetry, announcements, and reviews representing a variety of views from lesbian, feminist, and gay communities, and from other social change movements affecting women.

301 Lesbian Voices.
San Jose, Calif.: R. Nichols in affiliation with the Lesbian Feminist Alliance of Santa Clara County. v. 1:3 (1975)- . Quarterly.

Magazine with articles, poetry, interviews, letters, publications, announcements, and ads.

302 Long Time Coming.
Montreal, Que., Canada. v. 3:1 (1975)- . Quarterly.

Canada's first lesbian paper. Contains news, feature articles, classifieds, letters, drop-in center listings, announcements.

303   Maiden Voyage.
       Boston, Mass.: Daughters of Bilitis. v. 1-7 (1970)-2:3 (1971). Monthly.

       On microfilm. Continued by *Focus*.

304   Majority Report.
       New York, N.Y.: Majority Report Co. v. 2:7 (1972), 3:10 (1974), 4:24 (1975)- . Biweekly.

       Tabloid reporting and analyzing local, national, and international feminist news. Contains feminist ads, announcements, radio-TV listings, events calendars for the New York City area.

305   Media Report To Women.
       Washington, D.C.: Donna Allen. v. 3:1 (1975)- . Monthly.

       Newsletter of facts, actions, ideas, philosophy; what women are doing and thinking about the communications media, including how they represent women to the public, women's media production, and the employment situations at individual companies. Covers women's issues in all forms of print and non-print media. Includes an annual index, and directory of women's media groups, library collections, bookstores, courses, and individual media women.

306   Momma: The Newspaper/Magazine for Single Mothers.
       Venice, Calif.: Momma. v. 1:4, 6 (1973); 2:1-2 (1974). Monthly.

       Tabloid issued by Momma, a single mothers' organization, containing articles of shared experiences and practical and theoretical concern not only to single women but to the women's movement generally, poetry, classifieds, and announcements.

307   Mom's Apple Pie.
       Seattle, Wash.: Lesbian Mothers' National Defense Fund. 1974- . Some issues missing. Bimonthly.

       Newsletter of a group trying to raise money for legal fees in court cases involving custody of children of lesbian mothers in the U.S. and Canada. Chiefly case descriptions.

308   Monthly Extract: An Irregular Periodical.
       Stamford, Ct.: New Moon Publications. v. 1:3 (1972)- .

Small magazine dealing exclusively with women's health and gynecological self-help, women controlled childbirth, abortion, self-help clinics, conferences.

309 Mother.
Stanford, Calif.: published by and for gay women. v. 1:1-3 (1971). Monthly.

Lesbian tabloid covering the California lesbian community. Contains news articles, feature items, ads, announcements, interviews. Title changed with 2:1 to *Proud Woman*.

310 Mother Lode.
San Francisco, Calif.: San Francisco Women's Liberation. v. 1-6 (1971-73). Bimonthly.

Feminist paper, each issue presenting a theme: poetry, lesbian mothers, medicine, family, women in prison, "Why I want a wife." Ceased publication.

311 Moving Out: Feminist Literary & Arts Journal.
Detroit, Mich.: a collective of women at Wayne State University. v. 2:1 (1972)- . Semiannual.

Magazine committed to the expression and development of the female aesthetic outside the male-dominated publishing and editorial scene. Issues present feature articles, fiction, poetry, graphics, photography, art, drama, media reviews, women's projects.

312 NOW Acts.
Chicago, Ill.: National Organization for Women. v. 4:3, 5:1, 6:1 (1971-73). Quarterly.

News magazine reporting on movement events, news of feminist concerns, NOW speeches and conferences, and chapter news.

313 New Directions For Women In Delaware.
Newark, Del. v. 2:2 (1974).

Tabloid of substantial coverage of women's issues in Delaware. Contains news items, legislative, political and educational trends, feature articles, reviews, ads, and directories.

314 New York Radical Feminists Newsletter.
New York, N.Y.: New York Radical Feminist Association. v. 1:3 (1971), 2:5 (1972). Monthly.

Contains announcements of events, entertainment, conference reports, short articles.

315 No More Fun and Games: A Journal of Female Liberation.
Somerville; Cambridge, Mass.: Cell 16. v. 106 (1968-73). Irregular.

Collections of fiction, poetry, and essays on many aspects of sexism, began in anger and rebellion and growing with the women's movement.

316 Off Our Backs.
Washington, D.C. v. 1:1 (1970)- . Some issues missing. Monthly.

Strong newspaper covering world feminist issues, lengthy reviews, poetry, art, bibliographies, letters, classifieds, feminist ads.

317 The Other Woman: Bimonthly Canadian Feminist Newspaper.
Toronto, Ont., Canada. v. 3:4 (1975)- . Bimonthly.

Tabloid written with Canadian priorities, but also covering issues and events of concern to all women: American and Canadian divisions within the movement; International Women's Year, gay rights; rape; women in Latin America; wages for housework; beauty contests; women in universities; music; theater; book reviews; and bibliographies.

318 Peace and Freedom.
Philadelphia, Pa.: U.S. Section, Women's International League for Peace and Freedom. v. 32:6 (1972). Monthly.

Four page tabloid of news of concern to the women's movement for peace.

319 Power of Women: Journal of the Power of Women Collective.
London, England. v. 1:1 (1974); 1:3 (1975).

Collection of articles on the domestic and working conditions of women shopkeepers, secretaries, and unemployed women. Emphasis is also on wages for housework.

320 Prime Time: For the Liberation of Women in the Prime of Life.
New York, N.Y.: Marjory Collins. v. 3:1 (1975). Monthly.

Newsletter by and for older women which is against both sexism and ageism. Includes articles, classifieds, ads, letters, and poetry.

321 Proud Woman.
Stanford, Calif.: Mother Publications. v. 2:1 (1972). Bimonthly.

Continuation of *Mother,* with coverage of interest to all women.

322 Quest: A Feminist Quarterly.
Washington, D.C. v. 1:1 (1974)- . Quarterly.

Journal of political analysis of feminist concerns. Each issue has a theme: process of change; money, fame, and power; selfhood; spirituality; future visions; theories of revolution; organizations and strategies. Poetry, graphics, ads included.

323 Rat.
New York, N.Y.: R.A.T. Women. no. 16, 17, 19-24 (1970-71); one "special issue" (1972). Biweekly.

Tabloid begun by men, taken over by women. Strong, lengthy articles with a feminist perspective on issues including the male domination of the new left movements (Venceremos Brigade, peace movement, etc.), abortion, gay liberation, the media, narcotics, Quebec separatists, Weather Underground, third world women.

324 Red Rag: A Magazine of Women's Liberation.
London, England. no. 8 (1975)- . Irregular.

British journal with articles on politics and the women's movement there and throughout the world.

325 Revision.
Storrs, Ct.: Storrs-Willimantic Women's Liberation. no. 1, 2 (1970).

Newsletter including articles and notices of local interest and of interest to women in any university community.

326 Room of One's Own: A Feminist Journal of Literature and Criticism.
Vancouver, B.C., Canada: Growing Room Collective. v. 1:1 (Spring, 1975)- . Quarterly.

Contains poetry, short fiction, reviews, and articles on topics which include women in science fiction, women poets, Canadian women, Japanese fiction, Latin American literature, individual writers, interviews, and notes on contributors.

327 The Second Page.
San Francisco, Calif. no.6 (Nov. 1971). Irregular.

Formerly *The Women's Page*. Angry tabloid with long essays on opportunis on the left (describing the terms revolutionary, Marxist philosopher, New University Conference, New American Movement, and the journals *Socialist Revolution* and *Woman's World*); opportunism in the GI movement; profile of Todd Gitlin; female professionals' rip-off of the women's movement; the Bay Area Institute.

328 The Second Wave: A Magazine of the New Feminism.
Boston, Mass.: Female Liberation. v. 1:1 (1971)- . Irregular.

Magazine of strongly written, informative, topical articles, fiction, poetry, bibliographies, book reviews, letters, and feminist ads.

329 Shrew.
London, England: Women's Liberation Workshop. v. 3:9 (1971); 4:1, 4:2 (1972). Monthly.

Each issue of this British tabloid is produced by a different Women's Liberation Workshop group: Night Cleaners Collective, Psychology Group, Haverstock Hill, etc. Articles are on present concerns, women in history, labor, psychology, media reviews, ads, directory.

330 Sibyl-child: A Women's Arts & Culture Journal.
Baltimore, Md.: Aphra Ben Press. v. 1:1 (1975)- . Quarterly.

Little magazine of articles, interviews, fiction, short plays, poetry, media reviews, graphics, ads.

331 Sister. The Monthly Newsletter of New Haven Women's Liberation.
New Haven, Ct.: Women's Center. v. 1:6 (1971)- . Some issues missing. Monthly.

Contains movement articles of national and local current interest, directories of women's groups, letters, and events calendar.

332 Sister Courage: Greater Boston's Independent Feminist News-journal.
Allston, Mass.: Sister Courage, Inc. v. 1:3, 2:1 (1976)- . Monthly.

Tabloid reporting on events and issues such as women and labor unions, feminist therapy, women in prison, forced sterilization, prostitution, feminist credit unions, Susan Saxe; publication announcements and reviews, ads, classifieds, calendars of events.

333 Sister News.
Storrs, Ct.: UConn Women's Center. v. 1:1 (1972)-3:1 (1974). Some issues missing.

Newsletter of projects and activities of the Women's Center; includes poetry, classifieds, letters, and brief articles of concern to UConn women.

334 Spectre.
Ann Arbor, Mich.: Spectre Collective of White Revolutionary Lesbians. no. 1-3, 5, 6 (1971-72). Bimonthly.

Newspaper reflecting many points of view on issues in the lesbian movement (movement "stars," publications, feminism, parents, abortion, macho), announcements, ads.

335 The Spokeswoman: A Crossroads of Communication for Women.
Chicago, Ill.: Karen Wellisch. v. 1:1 (1970)-   . Monthly.

Independent newsletter reporting on local and federal court cases, legislative and organizational activity involving women's employment and health, news of women's labor organizing, insurance coverage, child care, finance, corporation affirmative action, and other trends and events. Includes book reviews, announcements, ads, and a section of job listings, primarily for professional and academic positions.

336 Tooth and Nail.
Berkeley, Calif.: Bay Area Women's Liberation. v. 1:4 (1970).

Articles in v. 1:4 include women's view of the Altamont rock festival, ageism, labor as a telephone operator, items by Alta.

337 Le Torchon Brule: Des Milliers de Femmes en Revolte.
Paris, France. no. 2, 3 (1972?). Monthly.

Serious and satirical tabloid of the French women's liberation movement. In French.

338 Union W.A.G.E.
Berkeley, Calif.: Union Women's Alliance to Gain Equality.
no. 11 (1972), 15 (1973), 23 (1974), 32 (1975), 33 (1976)- .
Bimonthly.

Tabloid chiefly with news of women's labor organizing and
union activity. Also includes news of women in other
countries, women prisoners, enforced sterilization, and other
issues, poetry, announcements, ads, letters.

339 Up from Under: By, for, and about Women.
New York, N.Y. v. 1:1 (1970)-1:5 (1973). Quarterly.

Magazine with articles of interest to all women, with emphasis
on working women; many in the style of shared experiences.
Includes some poetry, bibliographies, feminist ads, artwork,
photography, book reviews.

340 Velvet Glove.
Livermore, Calif.: Velvet Glove Press. no. 7 (1972).

Contains short fiction, poetry, articles, anecdotes,
photographs and artwork, and ads, supporting the liberation
of women. No. 7 also contains some work by male prisoners.

341 The Woman Activist: An Action Bulletin for Women's Rights.
Falls Church, Va.: Flora Crater. v. 3:7 (1973). Monthly.

Two page mimeo sheet reporting on court cases and legislative
action.

342 The Woman Offender Report.
Washington, D.C.: National Resource Center on Women
Offenders. v. 1:1-4 (1975). Bimonthly.

Newsletter reporting on national, state, and local issues and
programs concerned with reform in the treatment of women
offenders. The Center is co-sponsored by two groups within
the American Bar Association.

343 Womankind.
Chicago, Ill.: Chicago Women's Liberation Union. v. 1:8, 1:10
(1972). Monthly.

Tabloid of news items, articles, ads, shared experiences, and
announcements of concern to women.

344 Womankind.
  Detroit, Mich. v. 1:2 (1971?).

  Tabloid of longer articles (accidental poisoning of children,
  masculine mystique, nutrition, children's liberation,
  abortion) and announcements.

345 Woman's World.
  New York, N.Y. [1:1], 1:2 (1971) Quarterly.

  Tabloid with articles on Youth Against War and Fascism
  attack on prostitution, skin magazines, Catholic Church,
  abortion, nursery schools, rape, Black women.

346 Women: A Journal of Liberation.
  Baltimore, Md.; New York, N.Y. v. 1:1 (1969)- . Quarterly.

  One of the earliest feminist magazines. Each issue has a theme
  (e.g., sexuality, new culture, international women, androgyny,
  cost of living) with articles, poetry, art, letters.

347 Women & Film.
  Berkeley, Calif.: Persistence of Vision, Inc. no. 1 (1972)- .
  three issues a year.

  Contains writings on the films and resources of the Women's
  Film Archive and Information Center, women's film festivals,
  interviews with women filmmakers, bibliographies, history,
  film and book reviews, analyses and criticism.

348 Women & Revolution: Journal of the Women's Commission of
  the Spartacist League.
  New York, N.Y.: Spartacist Pub. Co. v. 1:1 (1971)- . Three
  issues a year.

  Feminist magazine from a viewpoint of Trotskyism,
  revolutionary Marxism. Articles on individual women like
  Emma Goldman; the condition of women of different
  countries, classes, races, and time periods; book reviews;
  league directories; and publications announcements.

349 Women Artists Newsletter.
  New York, N.Y. v. 1:7 (Dec. 1975).

  Newsletter with items on women artists, past and present, and
  women in the art world. Includes calendar of one-woman
  and group shows and events, book reviews, ads.

350   Women for Armed Revolution.
      Oakland, Calif.: Woman's Liberation. no. 1-3 (ca. 1971).

      Magazine calling for socialist revolution and an autonomous
      anti-imperialist women's movement. Discusses working class
      women and third world women.

351   Women in Libraries.
      New York, N.Y.: ALA/SRRT Task Force on Women. v. 4:4
      (1975)-   . Bimonthly.

      Reports on activities, meetings, and resources of concern to
      women librarians and pertaining to feminist programs and
      materials in libraries.

352   Women Library Workers.
      San Francisco, Calif.: Women Library Workers. [special issue]
      (1975)-   .

      Newsletter of an organization begun to "combine the energies
      of credentialed and non-credentialed women to change the
      existing distribution of power in libraries."

353   Women Strike For Peace. Memo.
      Washington, D.C. v. 4:2 (1965)-5:1 (1966). Monthly.

      Newsletter of a national group of women, many of whom had
      sons in Vietnam and who organized to do all that they could to
      end the war and the arms buildup. Contains photos, news of
      anti-war demonstrations, politicians, peace movement visits to
      Vietnam.

354   Women Strike For Peace. W.S.P. Newsletter.
      New York, N.Y. v. 1:2 (1968). Quarterly.

      Brief reports of anti-war activities of W.S.P. and other groups;
      short articles.

355   Women Today.
      Washington, D. C.: Today Publications & News Service, Inc.
      v. 1:1 (1971)-   . Biweekly.

      Newsletter reporting on the latest federal, state, and local
      legislative activities, reports, hearings, programs, and court
      cases, activities of national and special interest groups and
      campus women's programs, announcements of new women's
      publications and conferences.

356   Women United: The Voice of Women United for Action.
New York, N.Y. v. 1:1-2 (1973).

Tabloid newsletter of an organization demanding fair food prices and price roll-backs, attacking ranchers, growers, markets, and the food processing industry.

357   Women's Equity Action League. WEAL Washington Report.
Washington, D.C. no. 1 (1971)- . Irregular.

Report on congressional activity compiled by the WEAL Legislative Committee. Detailed current reporting on bills and other legal and governmental activities affecting women. Important research aid. Supplement to *Women Today*.

358   Women's Liberation of Michigan Monthly.
Detroit, Mich. v. 1:7 (1970); 2:4-7 (1971). Monthly.

Mimeographed newsletter with articles of political and social concern, national and local news items, legislative reporting, poetry, events. Previously called *Coalition*.

359   Women's National Abortion Action Coalition. WONAAC Newsletter.
New York, N.Y. 11 issues (1971-72). Monthly.

Newspaper of local and national legislative and organizational trends and events affecting abortion, contraception, and sterilization laws.

360   The Women's Page.
San Francisco, Calif. 1 issue suppl. to *It Ain't Me Babe*: v. 1:1 (1970). Irregular.

Tabloid expressing strongly many of the major concerns of the movement in 1970. Several angry items discuss women oppressing women.

361   Women's Press.
Eugene, Ore.: Women's Center. v. 1:13, 2:4 (1972). Monthly.

Tabloid of local and national news, poetry, features (including the politics of touch and an issue put together by lesbians), ads, and announcements.

362   Women's Rights Law Reporter.
New York, N.Y. v. 1:1-2 (1971-72). Quarterly. Subscription held by the UConn Law School Library, West Hartford.

Substantial magazine of articles to aid women's lawyers on legal rights pertaining to education, birth control, abortion, employment, domestic relations, incarceration, women in the legal profession, criminal law, constitutional law. Also contains book reviews, poetry.

363   Women's Voices.
Buffalo, N.Y.: Sub Board I, Inc., SUNYAB. v. 2:3 (1974).

Vol. 2, no. 3 presents women in the arts. Includes one-page bibliography "In Search of a Feminist Aesthetic."

364   The Working Mother: The Voice of Mothers' and Children's Liberation.
New York, N.Y.: Maternal Information Services. v. 1:2 (1971). Quarterly.

Twelve-page newsletter reporting on trends, incidents of discrimination, anecdotes, and publications in support of liberating mothers and their children.

AUTHOR INDEX

TITLE INDEX

SUBJECT INDEX